Turning Points

Vaughan Roberts

Authentic

First published in 1999 by OM Publishing
Reprinted 1999, 2000, 2001, 2002
Reprinted in 2003 by Authentic Lifestyle

12 11 10 09 08 07 06   13 12 11 10 9 8 7

Reprinted 2006 by Authentic Media,
9 Holdom Avenue, Bletchley, Milton Keynes, Bucks., MK1 1QR
and 129 Mobilization Avenue, Waynesboro, GA 30830-4575, USA
www.authenticmedia.co.uk

British Library Cataloguing in Publication Data
A catalogue record for this book is available from the British
Library

ISBN 1-85078-336-5

Cover design by Sam Redwood
Print Management by Adare Carwin
Printed in Great Britain by J.H. Haynes & Co., Sparkford

Turning Points

To Tom, James, Katie, Alice and George

Contents

Acknowledgements

I am grateful to David Gibb and Clare Heath-Whyte for reading the manuscript, to David Anthony for providing the diagram and to all who have attended "The Ebbe's Tavern" at the "Parrot" – their questions and comments stimulated much of the thinking that led to this book.

Introduction

"History is bunk": The famous words of Henry Ford during his libel suit with the *Chicago Tribune* in 1919. Was he right? There has been much debate in recent decades over the nature of history. Is there a pattern to it? Is it heading somewhere? Or is it nothing but a random series of disconnected events?

Not long ago one of the most popular versions of the view that history is ordered was that of the Marxists. They observed a clear pattern: an inevitable progression from one cycle to another. Feudalism was replaced by capitalism and socialism in turn, before the great ideal of communism was reached: everyone voluntarily contributing to the needs of others. "From each according to his abilities, to each according to his needs." That was the goal to which everything was seen to be heading: a great, united, global society of equals.

It was a noble vision. But the history of the twentieth century has shown it to be an impossible dream. Changes in social structures cannot change the selfishness within. The great communist revolutions have not achieved the Utopia they promised. Instead they have brought corruption and misery. We have seen too much

over the last few decades to be idealists any more. There
are few visionaries around these days; just cold-headed,
cynical realists.

That cynicism is reflected in our modern views of history. There is very little sense of order or progress. Take,
for example, the so-called "Cleopatra's nose" theory of
history. What was it that ultimately led to Mark
Antony's downfall – an event that was to have repercussions for the whole Roman Empire? The answer,
according to the theory, is Cleopatra's nose! Antony was
infatuated by her beauty and by her nose in particular.
And that infatuation was the beginning of the end for
him. So, the argument goes, there is no pattern to history. It is completely random, governed by chance
events. If Cleopatra's nose had had a bump in the middle or a large boil on it, everything would have been different. And the conclusion is: there is no point in trying
to learn anything from history. There is no order to it. We
can not predict what will happen. We are just victims of
fate. History is governed by chance – freak events like
Antony's infatuation with Cleopatra's nose.

Is history ordered or random? That might sound like
an obscure and irrelevant academic debate, but in fact it
has profound relevance for each one of us. It takes us to
some of the most important questions we can ever ask.
Is there a meaning to life? Where is it all heading? What
is the point of it all? Is human history a random process
going nowhere? Or is it under control – heading towards
a goal, a destination? And what about my life? How
does it fit in? Does it have a point?

The beginning of a new millennium is an obvious
time to ask such questions. It is true that 1 January 2000
was one day like any other. It had no significance in and
of itself. But then nor do our eighteenth or twenty-first
or sixtieth birthdays and yet we often mark them in

some way. They provide landmarks in our lives; stage-posts which give us an opportunity to look back and review the past and then to look ahead and think about the future. The new millennium affords a similar opportunity to humanity as a whole. It is no surprise that it has been marked by the publication of a number of histories of the world. But will such histories help us to answer the big questions of life? It all depends . . . We are back to our earlier question. Does history make sense? Is it heading anywhere?

The Christian answer is a confident "Yes". The Bible claims that this world had a definite beginning and will have a definite end. God has a plan for human history and it is focused on a person: Jesus of Nazareth. H.G. Wells, an atheist, once wrote: "I am a historian, I am not a believer, but this penniless preacher from Galilee is irresistibly the centre of history." Jesus' massive impact on both individuals and civilizations over the centuries is not in doubt. One writer put it well: "I'm far within the mark when I say that all the armies that ever marched, and all the navies that ever sailed, and all the parliaments that ever sat, and all the kings that ever reigned, put together, have not affected the life of man upon earth as has that one solitary life."

What do you make of him? Could it be that this extraordinary man belongs not just to the past but to the present and the future as well? Could he be the centre of history, as the Bible claims; the one who makes sense of life? Perhaps you are a sceptic. You suspect that the Bible is little more than Christian propaganda which cannot be taken seriously as an historical source. This book has been thrust into your hands by an earnest friend and you do not really want to read it. You find it hard to believe that a distant figure from the first century could have much relevance today. But what if he does, as millions in our world believe? Go on – keep reading! You have nothing to lose and – you never know – you might have much to gain.

We will be looking at the key turning points of history as outlined in the Bible. The ambitious goal is to go from creation to the end of the world in a few short pages – a history of the world in nine chapters. It will not read like a normal history book. There will be no mention of the great battles and emperors of whom we learnt at school. This book will not help you pass finals papers or score extra marks in a pub quiz. But it aims to do something far more important: to help you see history as God sees it so that you might fit in with his plans for the world. It will leave you with a choice. You might remain unconvinced and decide to continue living as before. But there is another possible outcome. I was in my last year at school when I first began to investigate Christianity. It began largely as an intellectual interest. It never occurred to me that it would make any difference to my life. But the more I studied, the more convinced I was that Jesus was alive and that he alone made sense of life. It was then, at the age of eighteen, that I began to follow him. My life was turned upside down and I have never regretted it. Who knows – perhaps what you read in this book will lead to a similar "turning point" in your life.

1

In the Beginning

A few years ago Jonathan Gabay faced, as he himself described it, "chaos, absolute darkest desolation. I felt literally on the edge of a cliff." That experience of deep depression led him to ask the age-old questions: "Why go on? What's the point? Is there meaning to life?" As time went by, the depression lifted but the questions remained and he began to write to famous people to see what answers they could give. The results of his research were published in 1995 in a book entitled *The Meaning of Life*. It does contain some wise words but, for the most part, it makes depressing reading as it becomes clear that very few of the celebrities have any idea what to say. Some make a brave attempt. There is Neil Kinnock's "Mutuality is the essence of life", whatever that means. Others adopt a classic diversionary tactic to avoid serious issues – they just laugh the whole thing off. Tony Husband, the cartoonist, writes "You do the hokey cokey – that's what it's all about." Alexei Sayle, the comedian, says "The meaning of life? – I don't know – but I do know the meaning of 'Eichhörnchen' – it's German for squirrel." Amusing maybe, but sad too. Have they got nothing better to say to a man who describes himself as "in chaos, absolute darkest desolation"? These issues are no joke – they are very serious for many people. Perhaps the most honest, and yet tragic, reply came from Sir Michael Hordern, the actor, writing only weeks before his death: "I am sorry but I see at the end of mine, no meaning to life but to fade into the light of the common day."

It was Plato, the Greek philosopher, who described man as "a being in search of meaning". For some it is a conscious quest that dominates their lives. Many of us prefer to suppress it, even laugh it off, perhaps because deep down we fear that it may lead nowhere – that, in the words of Edmund Blackadder (not a famous philosopher!): "Life is like a broken pencil – pointless." We are surrounded by people who suffer from what has been called "Marie Antoinette's disease" because she first coined the phrase that sums it up so well: "Nothing tastes". Everything seems so bland and meaningless. People everywhere are crying out inwardly: "There must be something more than this; something that will give meaning and purpose to life." They look all over for satisfaction, for some water that will quench their spiritual thirst.

What do you live for?

Some look to money and possessions. Their whole lives are dominated by the desire to accumulate. Nearly 750,000 Britons are addicted to shopping, according to a report by the Economic and Social Research Council. One man they interviewed said: "The only way to stop being depressed is to go shopping – but then it only comes back later." Another added: "It's like time stands still when I am shopping." The title of a recent book by

Mike Starkey provides a sad summary of the lives of many: *Born to Shop*. He comments: "In an earlier age life's adversity was met by a robust faith, even if it was only in human nature. Today we have our own solution. When the going gets tough, the tough go shopping." "If only I won the lottery and could afford a bigger house, a faster car, more exotic holidays, then all would be well." But would it? John D. Rockefeller, one of the richest men of the twentieth century, was once asked, "How much money does it take for someone to be really satisfied?" He replied: "Just a little bit more." Most of us know the truth of that. We have seen enough miserable millionaires to know that money and possessions are not the key to a fulfilling life, but we still pursue them. Why is that? A recent analysis in *Time* magazine is very shrewd: The 1970s was the "Me Decade", when introspection ruled. The 1980s was the "My Decade", when materialism ruled. The 1990s became the "Post-My Decade", when materialism still ruled but only because we did not know what to put in its place.

Others look to sex and relationships to satisfy the thirst within. Of course they can provide great pleasure, but so often they add to our confusion rather than increasing our security. The old morality has been rejected; anything goes. George Michael summed up the current mood in an interview with *The Big Issue* in 1998: "The only moral involved in sex is whether it is consenting or not." Without the guidelines of the past, many young people do not know where to turn in this area of their lives. One first-year student described her experiences in a university flat: "There are five of us, all girls. One regularly has casual sex with guys she picks up at clubs, one is a practising lesbian and one has a boyfriend who stays here virtually all the time. In the first term one of us had an abortion, two took the morning-after pill. I just don't know how to cope with all this."[1]

Even if everything starts well, we do not seem able to make our relationships last. We live in a throw-away culture. When the toaster stops working we just throw it away and get the new model. We do the same with lovers, which leaves many people feeling as if they are on the scrap heap – more empty than they felt before. In July 1996, 150 "Quick Court" kiosks were ceremonially unveiled in Arizona, USA. Press a button and a voice speaks: "Are you absolutely certain this marriage can't be saved?" Press "Yes" and divorce papers are printed out. "So in the time it takes to order a pepperoni pizza, your marriage has been terminated. Quick Court can't actually grant a divorce, but most cases are 'no-fault divorces' which simply require a judge to rubber stamp the decision."[2] The problem of divorce is just as acute in Britain. We have become the divorce capital of Europe with one in three marriages breaking up; two in three in London. Every year about 150,000 children become the victims of their parents' divorces. No wonder that an increasing number of younger people are suspicious of marriage and prefer to cohabit or stay single instead.

There are still others who look to ambition and success – that's what they live for. They have their sights set on some goal they long to achieve: a first-class degree; a place in that team; promotion at work. But, so often, when the goal is achieved and the initial euphoria passes, it leaves us just the same as we were before. I will never forget the conversation I had with John that summer term. We had not spoken before, but he approached me in the canteen queue with the words, "You're a Christian aren't you?" When I told him that I was he said, "I am an atheist." It was clear that that was an invitation to talk so I asked him, "Do you want me to try to persuade you that Christianity is true?" He did, and we talked for a couple of hours. He was interested but left unconvinced. We never spoke again. Two weeks later he was dead. He killed himself the day after discovering that he had got a first in his end-of-year exams. He found that the achievement of his ambition did not bring ultimate satisfaction. Peter Sellers put it well: "The expectation is greater than the realisation."

Pleasure is just as transitory. Someone once said: "Happiness is a cigar called Hamlet: it goes up in smoke." And yet still the pursuit of pleasure is the driving force in many lives. Jackie Collins, the novelist (if I can flatter her with that title) once summed up her aim in life with these words: "You can be fourteen or forty-five, but you'll never know when your life is going to end – so you really must enjoy every day, every minute. Live life – that's my motto."[3] Jeff Goldblum, the actor, lives according to a similar philosophy: " 'Live and love' is how I organise my life. In fact it is not only a part of my teaching and acting but my chief endeavour. Get the banality out of the way, put on your clothes and have fun."[4] But so often those who worship pleasure end up disillusioned. It fails to deliver what it promises. What was at first an intoxicating experience soon appears dull and has to be replaced by a greater "high". Life becomes a tantalizing search for the ultimate experience which is always just beyond our reach. It is what the philosophers call the "hedonistic paradox". John Stuart Mill understood it by bitter experience. After preaching the pursuit of happiness for years he came to understand that "this end [happiness] was only to be attained by not making it the direct end. For those are only happy . . . who have their minds fixed on some object other than their own happiness."[5]

Reverend Stephen Pullen, a vicar in Bedfordshire, caused a national uproar in January 1995 when he wrote in his parish magazine that "a complete ignorance of the things of God unites 95 per cent of the parish who live out their sordid little lives without any reference to God." Libby Purves responded in *The Times*;

> The accusation of having a 'sordid little life' probably hits a more raw nerve today than at any other time in history. For, now that so many of us have given up on the afterlife, we are very touchy about whether we are making the most of our earthly one. The phrases of the age are 'quality of life'; 'live life to the full' and 'lifestyle'. The worst insult is 'get a life'. We pore over newspaper day-in-the-life-of celebrities and wonder whether we would be better off if we moved to the country, went to the gym, or dressed only in white and ate raw celery . . . We scheme to get a few extra years and then worry about whether we will enjoy them. Meanwhile, we are uncomfortably aware that our daily lives are a bit short on intimations of immortality, so we seize on anything which promises a quick glimpse of the Beyond: it could be sex and drugs and rock 'n' roll, an exercise adrenalin high, a dose of sloppy diluted Buddhism, a mantra, an isolation tank . . . Anything to disguise from ourselves the fact that, secretly, most of us are afraid that we do indeed lead 'sordid little lives' . . . So accuse us of 'sordid little lives' at your peril, vicar. The reason we get so cross is that we *know* they are sordid. We are all, when we can spare the time from the mean, coarse, squalid, selfish business of getting through the day, looking for a way out and up.[6]

I found that a remarkably honest article. The vicar may not have been very tactful when he described his parishioners as living "sordid little lives", but he was onto something. It is what I am saying in a slightly different way. Many people are spiritually thirsty. We go to great lengths to try to satisfy that thirst but all the water in the world around us, that promises so much, is like salt water: "Water, water everywhere nor any drop to drink." "I can't get no satisfaction" – it could almost be the anthem of our age. Why is it that money, sex, ambition, pleasure, and all the other things that we run after, do not ultimately satisfy us? The Bible's answer is very clear: it is because our thirst is not caused by the lack of such things. It is caused rather by the break-up of our relationship with God.

Meaning and origin

This leads us back to the big question with which this chapter began: what is the meaning of life? Does our existence have a purpose? That all depends on our origin: were we created, or did we just come into existence by chance?

Some children were playing one day when they came across two bits of wood. They took them to their father and asked him, "What are they for, Daddy?" The father picked them up and looked at them. The first was just an ordinary stick that had fallen down from a tree. It bore no signs of human workmanship. So the father said, "This bit of wood isn't for anything in particular." The second piece of wood was different. The father noted that it had smooth edges and patterns on it and a perfectly symmetrical hole at the top. Common sense told him that this had not all happened by chance. It had been worked on by a skilled craftsman. To answer his children's question he had to discover the intention of its maker: what did he have in mind as he carved it? It did not take him long to work out – he was holding a candlestick.

To discover whether or not human life has a purpose, we are bound to consider the question of our origin. In the end there are only two options – either this world was created, or it began by chance. Did we simply come into existence by accident like that first bit of wood? If so we must say, like the father, that human life "isn't for anything in particular". The concept of purpose does not make sense without a creator. Steven Weinber wrote one of the earliest accounts of the Big Bang. He argued that the universe came into existence as a result of a purely coincidental amalgamation of different chemicals. The consequence was both obvious and depressing: "The more the universe seems comprehensible, the more it seems pointless." Human life is simply "a more or less farcical outcome of a chain of accidents." [7] Is that it? Do we have to conclude with Jean-Paul Sartre that life is ultimately meaningless: "Here we are, all of us, eating and drinking to preserve our precious existence and . . . there is nothing, absolutely no reason for existing"?

The Christian answer is a firm "No". We come now to the first crucial event in the history of the world according to the Bible. Hendrik van Loon began his history of the world with these words: "We live under the shadow of a gigantic question mark. Who are we? Where do we come from? Whither are we bound? Slowly, but with persistent courage, we have been pushing this question mark further and further towards that distant line, beyond the horizon, where we hope to find our answer. We have not gone very far." [8] How different from the Bible. It begins, not with questions, but with a confident declaration: "In the beginning God created the heavens and the earth." [9] It is just presented as a fact. There was a time when God alone existed. There was nothing for him to work on; he made everything out of nothing – he just said the word and the universe came into existence. Everything that exists has been made by him. That includes us: "So God created man in his own image, in the image of God he created him; male and female he created them."[10] If that is true, we are close to discovering the mystery of the meaning of life. The carving on the bit of wood presented to the father pointed to a workman – it was not just an accident. And the workman made it for a purpose: to hold candles. The mind of the creator reveals the purpose of the created. Surely it is the same for us? If we want to know what life is all about, we must discover what God had in mind when he made us.

Did God make the world?

But before we consider God's purpose in making us we must dwell for a moment on the claim that he made the world. How can we be so sure? Hasn't modern science disproved the book of Genesis with its account of creation? Surely we should leave such mythical beliefs behind and stick with the facts?

The "conflict" between science and religion has been greatly overstated. In 1916 James Leuba surveyed 1000 scientists in the USA and found that about 40 per cent believed in God. He predicted that this percentage would diminish as knowledge increased. But when the survey was repeated 80 years later it produced almost identical results.[11] Many of the world's leading scientists continue to be deeply committed believers who see no conflict between their studies and their faith. For example, Sir John Houghton, formerly professor of atmospheric physics at Oxford University, has written:

I agree with some of the great scientists in the early days of the scientific revolution 300 years ago who spoke of two books of God's revelation – the Book of Nature from which we learn about God's creative activity in the Universe, and the Book of God's Word, the Bible, from which we particularly learn of God's revelation of himself in Jesus. The views from these two books complement and support each other rather like the effect we experience when viewing through binoculars or through a stereoscope. A view with a single eye is flat, but with both eyes depth and perspective is added.[12]

Science and religion are two different ways of looking at the world; complementary rather than contradictory. Science is limited to the "How?" and "When?" questions. The Bible has little to say in answer to them – it is not designed to be a scientific text book. It is more concerned with other questions: "Who?" and "Why?". "Who made the world and for what purpose?" That is the focus of the first chapter of the Bible. It is not designed to give us a scientific account of how the world began; it has been written to make a theological point: "God made the world." Doesn't our observation of the world around us prompt us to agree? The design on the candlestick pointed to a craftsman who made it. Surely the amazing intricacy of nature points to the same conclusion? Think of the human eye, for example. David Watson has written: "A television camera has 60,000 photo-electric elements which enable it, in a limited sense, 'to see'. But the marvellous human eye, which focuses automatically, sees in all weather, and normally functions unceasingly for 70 or more years, contains more than 137,000,000 elements." Or the ear: "A grand piano has 240 strings by which a gifted musician can produce beautiful sounds. But the tiny human ear which enables us to listen to those sounds and appreciate their beauty consists of 24,000 strings!" Could such things really have come into existence by accident?[13]

This "argument from design" has been challenged in recent years. Professor Richard Dawkins of Oxford University is one amongst many who insist that the intricacy of the world does not point to a creator: it can all be explained by evolutionary theory. But even if one accepts that theory, what began the process in the first place? Charles Darwin himself said once: "I cannot believe with my mind that all this was created by chance." George Kinoti, professor of zoology at the University of Nairobi, spends his days studying nature. He has written: "The complexity, incredible ordering and beauty of the biological world speak, I am convinced, of a wise and powerful Creator. Like the heavens mentioned in the Psalms of the Bible, the living world testifies eloquently to the Creator."[14] It does not amount to QED proof, of course, but the world around us is a powerful pointer to the invisible God who was the "first cause" of it all.

The argument has been strengthened in recent years by the discoveries of cosmologists. They have noticed a series of remarkable "coincidences" which all combine to make human life possible. Tiny changes in the universal constants, such as gravity, the velocity of light and nuclear forces, would make our existence impossible. Professor John Polkinghorne, President of Queens' College, Cambridge makes the point powerfully:

> In the early expansion of the universe there has to be a close balance between the expansive energy (driving things apart) and the force of gravity (pulling things together). If expansion dominated then matter would fly apart too rapidly for condensation into galaxies and stars to take place. Nothing interesting could happen in

so thinly spread a world. On the other hand, if gravity dominated the world would collapse in on itself again before there was time for the processes of life to get going. For us to be possible requires a balance between the effects of expansion and contraction which at a very early epoch in the universe's history (the Planck time) has to differ from equality by not more than 1 in 10^{60}. The numerate will marvel at such a degree of accuracy. For the non-numerate I will borrow an illustration from Paul Davies of what that accuracy means. He points out that it is the same as aiming at a target an inch wide on the other side of the observable universe, twenty thousand million light years away, and hitting the mark![15]

"Coincidences" such as this are collectively referred to as the "Anthropic Principle": "We live in a universe whose constitution is precisely adjusted to the narrow limits which alone would make it capable of being our home."[16] This suggests very powerfully that the universe did not arise simply by chance but was the product of a divine designer.

Some scientists have avoided this conclusion by suggesting that there is a huge number of universes in addition to our own, each operating according to its own laws. The vast majority do not have the right conditions for life, but the occasional freak universe, such as our own, is different, as one would expect – from an infinite number of "attempts" the odd one is bound to hit the jackpot sooner or later. But there is no evidence of other universes beyond our own; the theory is pure speculation. Russell Stannard, professor of physics at the Open University has commented: "This suggestion is not science . . . If people prefer to interpret the cosmos that way, rather than accept a designer God, then that has to be their choice. As far as I am concerned, there is little doubt that where the Anthropic Principle is concerned, believers are in pole position."[17]

Once again it is not QED proof, but these combined "arguments from design" are powerful pointers to the existence of a divine creator. And what of the pointers that we find within ourselves? Take conscience, for example. Whether we like it or not, we all have an innate sense of right and wrong planted deep within us. The fact that the same core values are shared by every society of every age suggests that this is not simply a product of social conditioning. A purely evolutionary view of the development of humanity does not explain it. George C. Williams, one of the most distinguished evolutionary biologists, has written that evolution is a system in which the message is always "exploit your environment, including your friends and relatives, so as to maximise your gene's success. The closest thing to a golden rule is 'Don't cheat', unless it is likely to provide a net benefit." [18] How can we explain the fact that all of us have a sense that such selfishness is not right? We may not live up to it, but we all have a nagging feeling within, an "altruistic impulse", that tells us that we should look to the interests of others. Where does that come from?

And what about the religious impulse? Religion has been a part of every society in history. Even when states, such as the communist regimes of this century, have tried to suppress belief in God they have not succeeded. The growth of the Christian church in China is a striking example. It is estimated that there were just over five million Christians there at the time of the Communist revolution in 1949. Missionaries were expelled and religion was discouraged but still the church has grown at a remarkable rate. By the 1990s there were about 80 million Christians in that country. The vast majority of people in the world still believe in some kind of god or gods and continue to do so even when they are in danger of persecution as a result. Why? What drives this impulse, which is also felt by many who would not identify with any particular faith? What prompts us to ask the big questions: "Who am I?"; "Where am I going?"; "What is life all about?"? Every other human desire is caused by a corresponding need which can be fulfilled. We are made in such a way that we need certain things to function properly. We need food and drink and if we do not get them we will die. Our experience of hunger and thirst point to those basic needs. Surely it is reasonable to suppose that there is a reason for our hunger and thirst for something that takes us beyond ourselves; for "spirituality"; for "God". Once again, a purely evolutionary account of human origins has no explanation for this phenomenon. Could it be that the oldest explanation is also the best – that this is one more pointer to the fact that we have been made by a loving Creator?

So what does it all mean?

We are back to the question of meaning again. What is life all about? Do you remember the two bits of wood the children took to their father? The question "What's it for?" does not make sense when applied to a stick that has just fallen from a tree – it is not "for" anything in particular. But when a piece of wood has been worked on by a craftsman it is possible to speak of meaning. Its purpose is that which was in the mind of its creator – to hold candles. Without a creator human life has no ultimate meaning. We just have to make sense of our own life in whatever way we can. We might as well invest as much as possible in money, sex, ambition, pleasure or whatever else we choose to live for, even if we know that they do not ultimately satisfy – there is nothing else. But if there is a creator, as the Bible insists and the world around us suggests, then we can conclude that life does make sense: we have been created for a purpose.

What is that purpose? What design was in God's mind when he made us? The book of Genesis reveals the Creator's plan. He made us "in his image". It is true that we human beings are part of the animal kingdom, but that is not all that we are. We are not just "naked apes", as Desmond Morris famously described us in the title of one of his books. God has set us above the rest of his creation as those who uniquely reflect his character. We are capable of creativity, altruism and conscience in a way that other creatures are not. Human beings alone, of all that God has made, are able to relate to him. That was his original plan for our lives: that we might live in his world in perfect relationship with him. The description of Adam and Eve in the Garden of Eden presents a picture of human life as it was designed to be. We are told that "God saw all that he had made and it was very good."[19] Human beings consciously submitted to God as their creator and enjoyed the perfect life as a result: harmony with their God leading to harmony with each other and the world around them.

If the Bible is right that we were created to live as God's friends, it is not surprising that we do not function properly unless that friendship is in place. We were designed in such a way that we need food and liquid if we are to survive, and we are hungry and thirsty until we get them. In a similar way we were designed to exist in a loving friendship with God. It is only in relationship with him that life ultimately makes sense and nothing other than that can bring lasting satisfaction. It was Augustine, the great church leader of the fifth century who once wrote: "Lord, you have made us for yourself and our hearts are restless till they find their rest in you."

We are, at last, able to give the Bible's answer to the searching questions of Jonathan Gabay with which this chapter began. "What is the meaning of life?" "What's the point of it all?" This world is not just an accident. God made it and had a plan for our lives. He designed us to relate to him as his friends. Most of us recognize that we do not live like that at the moment. The good news of Christianity is that Jesus Christ came to restore that friendship. He said:

> Come to me, all you who are weary and burdened, and I will give you rest.[20]
>
> I am the bread of life. He who comes to me will never go hungry, and he who believes in me will never be thirsty.[21]
>
> If anyone is thirsty, let him come to me and drink.[22]

A History of the World

The story so far:

1) Creation

Notes

1. UCCF "Briefing Paper" no. 2, *Student Sexuality* (Leicester, 1998).
2. *The Sunday Times*, 11-2-96.
3. *Annabel*, June 1993.
4. *The Sunday Times*, 16-5-93.
5. Quoted in Michael S. Horton, *The Law of Perfect Freedom* (Moody Press, 1993), 59.
6. *The Times*, 16-1-95.
7. Russell Stannard, *Doing Away with God* (Marshall Pickering, 1993), 80.
8. Hendrik van Loon, *The Story of Mankind* (Pocket Books Edition, 1942), 3.
9. Genesis 1:1.
10. Genesis 1:27.
11. *Nature*, April 1997.
12. Mike Poole, ed., *God and the Scientists* (C.P.O., 1997), 7.
13. *Is Anyone There?* (Hodder, 1979) 27.
14. Poole, ed., *God and the Scientists*, 4.
15. John Polkinghorne, *One World* (SPCK, 1986), 57.
16. Ibid.
17. Stannard, *Doing Away with God*, 100–101.
18. Quoted in an article by Alasdair Palmer in The *Sunday Telegraph*, 6-4-97.
19. Genesis 1:31.
20. Matthew 11:30.
21. John 6:35.
22. John 7:37.

2

Where It All Went Wrong

Imagine that you see an old man begging in the street. He is very dirty, wearing ragged clothes, and is obviously drunk. That is always a sad sight, but somehow it is even sadder once you learn that a few years ago he was a very distinguished professor in the local university. A man who had once had a position of prestige and authority has been reduced to a beggar. How are the mighty fallen!

We are looking at the key turning points in the history of the world as seen from the Bible's perspective. The first chapter took us to the beginning of everything: the creation. Humankind was introduced as the pinnacle of that creation, made in God's image and placed above everything else. There is no more exalted position on earth. But it was not long before everything went terribly wrong and we fell very low. That is the theme of the next great event of history, known for generations as "the Fall". The exalted humanity of God's creation becomes a shadow of its original self and the whole universe is affected.

There is a striking section in the film *Good Morning Vietnam*. Robin Williams plays an American forces DJ.

During his show one day he plays Louis Armstrong's great song "What a wonderful world". You will have heard it if you ever listen to *Desert Island Discs* – it appears almost as often as "My Way". At the very moment that the song begins, the cameras shift away from the DJ's studio to the world outside. The pictures on the screen tell a very different story from the words of the song. There are scenes from Vietnam: napalm destroying whole villages, children on fire – screaming in agony with terror written all over their faces, and all the time Louis sings on, "I see trees of green and skies of blue . . . And I say to myself, what a wonderful world, what a wonderful world."

It is a very poignant image. Yes – it is a wonderful world; a world that a loving God has made. And yet alongside all the beauty, all that is good, there is much that is very bad. It is a world in which we human beings seem intent on destroying each other – through warfare, economic injustice, crime and much more. It's tragic, and something within us tells us: "It shouldn't be like this." We're left asking, "What has gone wrong with our world?" It is a question that has been very much in the public domain for several years. The Jamie Bulger case, Dunblane, the atrocities in Northern Ireland and the attacks on the World Trade Centre in New York, have all contributed to cause a bout of national soul-searching. "What has spoilt this wonderful world of ours?" "Why do such things happen?" "Is there anything we can do to prevent their recurrence?"

In the 1970s Jacob Brownowski wrote a famous book called *The Ascent of Man*. The title sums up the optimism of many earlier this century. History was seen as the story of the progress of humanity. In one sense, of course, that is what it is. The last two thousand years have seen astonishing advances in our knowledge and capabilities. That progress has accelerated faster in the last century than in any other. Who would have thought in 1900 that by the next millennium we would have put men on the moon, transplanted hearts from one human to another and broadcast the same event simultaneously to millions in every continent on earth? But can we really talk of our "ascent"? In 1998 a national newspaper invited its readers to suggest words that sum up the century. "Television", "technology" and "computer" were in the top ten, but so were "holocaust" and "genocide".[1] A schoolgirl wrote in a history essay: "Armistice was signed on November 11, 1918, and since then we have had two minutes of peace once a year." It might have been a slip of the pen, but it conveyed a sad truth. More have died in wars in this century than in all the others put together. The century that has produced such progress has also brought us Hitler, Stalin and Pol Pot.

What hope can we have as we enter the next millennium? Will things really change if we manage to improve education, health care and political institutions? A quick look at our history would suggest not. Despite great progress in all these areas over many years, the same old problems continue to surface. No superficial solution will ever work because the fundamental problem does not lie on the surface: it goes very deep; it is a problem that lies within. Winston Churchill was surely right when he spoke these solemn words in the House of Commons in 1950:

> Man in this moment of his history has emerged in greater supremacy over the forces of nature than has ever been dreamed of before. He has it in his power to solve quite easily the problem of natural existence. He has conquered the wild beasts, and he has even conquered the insects and the microbes. There lies before

him, if he wishes, a golden age of peace and progress. All
is in his hand. He has only to conquer his last and worst
enemy – himself.

That is an enemy that over many centuries we have
proved ourselves quite incapable of defeating. It is true
that we have great dignity as those who have been made
in the image of God. We can perform wonderful feats of
creativity, bravery and selflessness. But there is another
side to our nature which goes just as deep. Robert Louis
Stevenson, the creator of Jekyll and Hyde, wrote: "I have
called my character Dr Jekyll and Mr Hyde. I could just
as well have called him Robert Louis Stevenson." We are
all capable of both good and evil, and no matter what we
do, we have never been able to remove the "Hyde" from
our personality. There was a series of letters in *The Times*
some years ago on the subject "What is wrong with the
world?" The shortest and most perceptive answer came
from the writer G.K. Chesterton: "Dear Sir, I am, Yours
sincerely, G.K. Chesterton". If we are honest with ourselves, can we seriously suggest that he is wrong?

Some respond by pointing the finger at God. If he
made us, surely he is to blame for the faulty design.
Spike Milligan has given powerful expression to that
point of view in his poem "Me", written in hospital during a time of depression: "If he says my sins are myriad
I will ask why he made me so imperfect. And he will say,
'My chisels are blunt'. I will say, 'Then why did you
make so many of me?' "[2]

Blaming God is an easy way out, but it does not satisfy many of us. We know that we are not machines,
programmed to behave in a certain way. We have a real
choice about how to live our lives. We are aware of the
difference between right and wrong and our conscience
tells us that we should do what is right. But again and

again we fail to do so and we only have ourselves to blame. There is something fundamentally wrong with us. Jesus said as much in debate with some religious Pharisees. They protested when he did not follow all their ceremonial practices. They were convinced, for example, that people made themselves dirty in God's sight when they ate "unclean" food. But Jesus pointed out that our problem goes far deeper than that:

> Don't you see that nothing that enters a man from the outside can make him 'unclean'? For it doesn't go into his heart but into his stomach, and then out of his body . . . What comes out of a man is what makes him 'unclean'. For from within, out of men's hearts, come evil thoughts, sexual immorality, theft, murder, adultery, greed, malice, deceit, lewdness, envy, slander, arrogance and folly. All these evils come from inside and make a man 'unclean'.[3]

The heart of the human problem is the problem of the human heart. The Bible tells us that it was not always like this. To understand what went wrong we must consider the next great turning point in the history of the world: "the Fall".

The Fall

The event described in the third chapter of the Bible has been dismissed as a quaint myth from the mists of time, irrelevant today. I hope that a closer look will reveal that such judgements are premature. We find in Genesis 3 the description of an event which provides a profound and relevant answer to the question with which we are concerned: "What has gone wrong with our world?" Opinions differ as to how literally the writer intends us to take this account. Are we meant to take the reference to the "tree of life" and the "tree of the knowledge of good and evil" as literal trees in the garden? And what about the speaking serpent? Did the author expect his readers to understand that he was really there in a literal sense talking to the woman, or is this simply a symbolic way of describing Satan? It seems to me that he describes a real event and yet uses a certain amount of symbolism as he does so. We must not allow such questions to distract us from the profound message that this section of the Bible contains.

The scene is set in chapter 2 of Genesis. We find humanity, represented by Adam and Eve, enjoying life in the Garden of Eden in perfect relationship with God. There is just one command: "You are free to eat from any tree in the garden; but you must not eat from the tree of the knowledge of good and evil for when you eat of it you will surely die."[4] But they disobeyed:

> Now the serpent was more crafty than any of the wild animals the LORD God had made. He said to the woman, "Did God really say, 'You must not eat from any tree in the garden'?" The woman said to the serpent, "We may eat from the trees in the garden, but God did say, 'You must not eat fruit from the tree that is in the middle of the garden, and you must not touch it, or you will die.'" "You will not surely die," the serpent said to the woman. "For God knows that when you eat of it your eyes will be opened, and you will be like God, knowing good and evil." When the woman saw that the fruit of the tree was good for food and pleasing to the eye, and also desirable for gaining wisdom, she took some and ate it. She also gave some to her husband, who was with her, and he ate it (Genesis 3:1–6).

Adam and Eve did what God had forbidden them to do. That, in a nutshell is their sin – they disobeyed God. But what is so bad about eating a bit of fruit? There is more going on here than that. It was not just that they ate some fruit. The essence of their sin was a desire to become like God. The snake tempts Eve by telling her: "If you eat of this tree you will be like God, knowing good and evil" (v. 5). That is a very attractive thought to Adam and Eve. They want to know good and evil – not in the sense that they want to know the difference between right and wrong. They already have a sense of that – how else could God blame them for disobeying him and eating from the tree? "Knowledge of good and evil" refers not to knowing the difference between what is right and wrong, but rather to *deciding* what is right and wrong. It is an act of blatant rebellion. God alone, as the creator, has the right to set the standards, but Adam and Eve are not prepared to accept his authority. They take the crown off his head and place it firmly on their own. They are telling God that from now on they will run their own lives their way.

This is not just ancient history. It involves us. The apostle Paul in the New Testament goes so far as to suggest that we were there.[5] Not, of course, in a crude literal sense. Rather, Adam was our representative. He represented us perfectly in the Garden. He did exactly what we would have done had we been there. The result was that the world and human beings have never been the same since. All of us follow quite naturally and willingly in the way of Adam and Eve. We repeat their sin every day of our lives: we are rebels against God.

I am not a great fan of modern classical music, but when some free tickets for a prom at the Albert Hall became available I was persuaded to take advantage of them. The music was as inaccessible as I had feared. It was the world premiere of a song cycle which went way over my head and I took the opportunity to catch up on a bit of sleep. I was wakened by rapturous applause – the rest of the audience was clearly more cultured than me. As the cheering continued the conductor beckoned to the wings for the composer to come on and take a bow. The triangle player, who had a very minor role in the piece, was sitting between the conductor and the composer's seat and thought that he was being invited to take the applause. He looked a bit confused but stood none the less and bowed. At that very moment the composer appeared on stage behind him and began to walk to the centre. The poor triangle player realized what had happened and sat down again with a very red face. It was the only truly enjoyable moment of the whole evening. The percussionist had made an innocent mistake, but we do something similar quite deliberately. God the creator is the great composer of everything. He should be centre stage in his world. But we push him out of the picture. We are determined to be at the centre and to take the bow. It is that attitude of independence and rebellion that is at the heart of the problems of the world.

It was a big shock to me when someone first explained what "sin" was according to the Bible. I had always assumed that the "sinners" were murderers, rapists and paedophiles; not me. I was fairly well behaved; I even watched *Blue Peter*. My parents liked me, the headmaster liked me, and I assumed that if there was a God he liked me too. But then I heard that we were all guilty of the great sin of rebellion against God. We are not all the same. Some are criminals and drug dealers; others of us are greedy, lustful, selfish, arrogant or proud. The symptoms may be different, but we all have the same disease. The more I thought about it, the more I knew that it was true. I had lived in God's world as if he did not exist. I did what I wanted when I wanted and God had hardly got a look in, if he got in the picture at all. He had given me everything I enjoyed: my friends and family, a beautiful world to live in, and much more, but I had never bothered even to say that little word "thanks". Instead I lived my life without reference to him. It was the sin described in the story of Adam and Eve. Are we not all the same?

The consequences of the Fall

The consequences of such disobedience are very clear from the account in Genesis. The writer describes the immediate effects:

> Then the eyes of both of them were opened, and they realised that they were naked; so they sewed fig leaves together and made coverings for themselves. Then the man and his wife heard the sound of the LORD God as he was walking in the garden in the cool of the day, and they hid from the LORD God among the trees of the garden. But the Lord God called to the man, 'Where are you?' He answered, "I heard you in the garden, and I was afraid because I was naked; so I hid." And he said, "Who told you that you were naked? Have you eaten from the tree from which I commanded you not to eat?" The man said, "The woman you put here with me – she gave me some fruit from the tree, and I ate it." Then the LORD God said to the woman, "What is this you have done?" The woman said, "The serpent deceived me, and I ate." (Genesis 3:7–13).

"The Fall" leads to a dislocation of all the proper relationships there should have been. That is certainly clear in the individual's relationship with his or herself. We are told earlier that "The man and his wife were both naked, and they felt no shame."[6] The writer's words after their sin tell a different story: "Then the eyes of both of them were opened, and they realised that they were naked; so they sewed fig leaves together and made coverings for themselves."[7] The serpent's promise of verse 5 is fulfilled. Their eyes are opened, but they hate what they see. Their sense of self-esteem is shattered. At the very core of their being is a knowledge of guilt and shame. They can no longer bear to face themselves or let others see them as they really are, so they hide. The same is true of us today. There is no such thing as the complete fully-integrated personality in our fallen world. As Mark Twain said once: "Man is the only animal that blushes . . . and that needs to blush."

The dislocation of relationships is seen too in our relationship with other people. It had been the perfect match, which is not surprising because God was the matchmaker – a marriage truly made in heaven. God had made Eve to be the perfect partner for Adam. It all began well. When he first saw his new wife he could not stop singing he was so happy. But it was not long before it all went wrong. The bickering had begun: "The woman you put here with me – she gave me some fruit from the tree and I ate it" (v. 12) – it's all her fault. As the old joke puts it: "Adam blamed Eve, Eve blamed the serpent, and the serpent didn't have a leg to stand on!" It is pass the buck time. Adam and Eve start arguing and human relationships are spoilt for ever. There has never been a perfect marriage or friendship since.

There are also implications for the relationship of humanity to the rest of the creation. God had appointed Adam and Eve to be his vicegerents over the world he had made. That was not a charter for the abuse of the natural world that has so often been inflicted on it. They were to be the stewards of God's treasured possession, responsible to him for how they treated it. The fact that human beings were set over the world meant that, in some mysterious way, it was bound up with them. When they rebelled against God, that had consequences for the rest of creation. From now on, God says, they will experience nature as a hostile force to be subdued and not as a friendly ally: "Cursed is the ground because of you; through painful toil you will eat of it all the days of your life. It will produce thorns and thistles for you."[8]

Most seriously of all, human rebellion against God spoils our relationship with him. The writer presents a wonderful picture of God "walking in the garden in the cool of the day". It is as if he had come down for his daily chat with his friends Adam and Eve. But this time they do not come out to join him. They are hiding – cowering behind the trees, hoping they will not be seen. That is how we humans behave towards God – we run from him. It is popular to see religion as rather like a game of hide-and-seek.

I love hide-and- seek. It is a great game to play with children. You give them 30 seconds to go and hide and then off you go to look for them. It is not hard to know where to start – the loud patter of feet gave the game away when they first ran off. There is a certain etiquette to the game. It is not done to go straight to the hiding place and find them immediately. It is expected that you start off in the wrong place, saying loudly as you enter: "I wonder if Tom is in the bathroom". That always prompts a fit of noisy giggles from under the bed in the next room (which is where Tom always hides). You then enter the bedroom, sounding slightly exasperated this time; "Where can Tom be?" You have hardly got the words out before there are more giggles and then a little boy appears grinning: "Here I am!" It is not exactly a taxing game.

And it is not meant to be. The adult who finds a brilliant hiding place and stays there stony silent for hours spoils all the fun. That is what we are tempted to think that God is doing. We have been patiently searching for him for years, but he is a spoilsport and stays hidden. It is the complete opposite of the truth. God in his great love is seeking: "The LORD God called to the man, 'Where are you?' " But we are frightened and ashamed and hide from him. It has always been the same. Even when God went to the greatest possible lengths to seek us out and sent his son to earth to look for us, we still hid. The apostle John comments in the New Testament: "This is the verdict: Light has come into the world, but men loved darkness instead of light because their deeds were evil."[9]

Disobedience against God seems to offer so much. It makes great claims: "You will be like God". But its effects are devastating. It dislocates our relationships with ourselves, other people, the world we live in, and God.

The judgement of God

So far God does not appear to be directly involved in the consequences of our disobedience against him. A machine never works well if it is not used according to the maker's instructions. If we choose not to live as God designed us to live, there are bound to be harmful results – they are just part of the natural cause and effect built into our world. But there is more than that here. Our rebellion against God also invites the active judgement of God.

God's judgement on Adam and Eve reveals how seriously he takes our rebellion against him: "The LORD banished Adam from the Garden of Eden . . . After he drove the man out, he placed on the east side of the Garden of Eden cherubim and a flaming sword flashing back and forth to guard the way to the tree of life."[10] God had made it clear that when they ate of the tree of the knowledge of good and evil they would die and that is what happens. They are expelled from the presence of God and experience for the first time the horror of spiritual death – separation from God which begins here on earth and continues for ever.

That, says the Bible, is what we all deserve. We have all turned away from God. Some do it very obviously. They walk out of God's front door and slam it in his face shouting loudly: "No one believes in all that nonsense any more!" Others do it more politely. They slink out of God's back door. They might believe in God, say their prayers, even go to church from time to time, but when the crunch comes they do what they want – they run their own life. We all do it. Can we really blame God for being angry?

That brings us to the end of our look at the chapter in the Bible that describes "the Fall". It makes depressing reading. I hope you agree that it is very profound. Is this not the world we see today? Yes, we still have the tune of the wonderful world that the loving creator made ringing in our ears. There are echoes of it all around us. But as we hear that tune we look into a world that has been spoilt – children screaming in agony, lonely people living in despair, husbands and wives at each other's throats, innocents massacred in Rwanda and Bosnia. Why? What has gone wrong? Genesis chapter 3 has given us the answer. *We* have gone wrong. We have rebelled against our maker and he has responded in righteous judgement. The exalted humanity that God made in his image has become the degraded humanity that we know today – still bearing God's image, and yet corrupted in every part of our being. And that has had disastrous consequences for the whole of creation. It is like your favourite record, if you still have such old fashioned things, with a scratch down the middle. You can hear the beautiful music, but it is flawed all the way through. We have proved ourselves incapable of doing anything to deal with the fundamental problem. No matter how many advances we make in the worlds of technology, education and healthcare, the human heart remains the same – a heart that rejects God. But the Bible insists that there is hope.

In the early 1970s the great painting by Reubens that hangs at the west end of King's College Chapel in Cambridge was vandalized by the IRA. A notice appeared next to it on the following day: "It is believed that this masterpiece can be restored to its original condition." This world is the masterpiece of God, with humanity as its pinnacle. We have been spoilt by our rebellion against him, but it is his plan to restore us and the whole of his creation. In his love he remains committed to us despite our rejection of him. There are hints of that even in the gloom of the description of "the Fall". We could hardly blame God if he washed his hands of us after the appalling way in which we have treated him, but he does not do that. He continues to call to us as he called to Adam: "Where are you?" He also makes a mysterious promise in the midst of some words to the serpent: "I will put enmity between you and the woman, and between your offspring and hers; he will crush your head and you will strike his heel."[11] There will be a continuing struggle between human beings and Satan, but it will not last for ever. "It is believed that this masterpiece can be restored to its original condition." There will be a man, born of a woman, who will destroy evil for ever ("he will crush your head"). From now on we are

Notes

[1] *The Times*, 14-3-98.
[2] Spike Milligan, *Small Dreams of a Scorpion* (Penguin, 1972), 28.
[3] Mark 7:18–20.
[4] Genesis 2:16–17.
[5] Romans 5:12.
[6] Genesis 2:25.
[7] Genesis 3:7.
[8] Genesis 3:17–18.
[9] John 3:19.
[10] Genesis 3:23–24.
[11] Genesis 3:15.

3

The God Who Is There

Jan Morris, the distinguished historian and travel writer, includes a chapter on religion in her book on my home town, Oxford. She describes the different religious activities and then concludes:

> Oxford looks a Christian city still – the organs play bravely, and the canons sweep through Tom Quad in their white and crimson, surplices blowing in the breeze; but sometimes I find it easy enough to fancy all these old temples shuttered and neglected, the cathedral a museum, the college chapels - lecture rooms, an art gallery in the crypt of St Peter's and only the faithful Samaritan left, busier than ever, over his telephone in Iffley Road.[1]

There is a poetic poignancy in those words – a sense of regret and yet inevitability about the demise of faith.

Matthew Arnold caught the mood a century ago in his poem "Dover Beach":

> The Sea of Faith
> Was once, too, at the full, and round earth's shore
> Lay like the folds of a bright girdle furl'd;

But now I only hear
Its melancholy, long, withdrawing roar,
Retreating to the breath
Of the night-wind down the vast edges drear
And naked shingles of the world.[2]

Arnold wrote at the height of the Victorian era. The tide
of secularism was advancing, pushed on by the waves of
the Industrial Revolution. But the sea of faith was
ebbing, and the poet saw no prospect of its return. As the
new century arrived many believed that religion would
soon be a relic of the past – there would be no room for
religious belief in the brave new world of science and
technology. Nietzsche even proclaimed with confidence:
"God is dead". But the obituaries were written too soon.
The idea of God has stubbornly refused to lie down.
Under the graffito " 'God is dead' – Nietzsche" on a university wall, a student has added the words: " 'Nietzsche
is dead' – God".

The age of what you might call "scientific fundamen-
talism" appears to be over. Not long ago many people
questioned anything that could not be proved by strict
scientific method. There was no room in their world-
view for the transcendent. That attitude is far less
common today. There is a new openness to all sorts of
beliefs from crystals to Buddhism, from astrology to
Christianity.

The fascination with the unexplained can be seen all
around us. On television there is Michael Aspel with
Strange but True, Carol Vorderman's *Mysteries*, and *The X
Files*. Then there are the films: *Independence Day*, which
grossed $200 million in three weeks, *Men in Black* I and II,
and *Contact*, in which Jodie Foster plays an astrophysicist
receiving messages from outer space. And what about
the enduring popularity of Uri Geller, the spoonbending

star of the 1970s who has recently made a comeback? A few seasons ago Reading Football Club actually paid him to use his supernatural powers for their benefit, but they did not gain an obvious advantage.

Most of us can remember where we were on 31 August 1997 when we first heard the tragic news of the death of Diana, Princess of Wales. The reaction of the nation revealed a deeply ingrained spirituality. In the week leading to her funeral many who had not been in churches for years went along to pray or just be silent. One writer commented about the events of those days: "It was as if the spiritual tectonic plates underpinning the superficiality of the modern age had moved and heaved and the world was shaken by a spiritual earthquake."[3] Another said that they had shown "a profound spiritual emptiness which people want to have filled."[4] Damian Thompson made a similar point in an article entitled "Diana and the Pursuit of the Millennium."[5] "The familiar nostrum that our society has become irreversibly secular now seems hopelessly wide of the mark." He went on to refer to a recent survey which showed that belief in telepathy, UFOs and ghosts is growing and that 17 million Britons use alternative therapy. We do not seem able to forget about God. Douglas Coupland speaks with characteristic honesty: "I must remind myself we are living creatures – we have religious impulses – we *must* – and yet into what cracks do these impulses flow in a world without religion? It is something I think about every day. Sometimes I think it is the only thing I should be thinking about."[6]

In the past it was so straightforward – you just believed what some organized religion told you to believe. But now we have rebelled against that spiritual straitjacket – we want to make our own decisions and not be dictated to by some external authority. The result has been a proliferation of different beliefs as individuals have expressed their freedom to choose for themselves. But our rejection of organized religion has also brought confusion. Where do we turn if we want to know what to believe? Who can tell us what God is like?

The surveys suggest that over 70 per cent of Britons still believe in God. But which God? The answer is that most of us do not know. We would like to. The interest in spirituality reveals the sense that many have that they need god – "someone out there" to believe in. Douglas Coupland's book *Life after God* describes a culture that seems at one level to have moved on from God. But he ends with these striking words:

> Now – here is my secret: I tell you with an openness of heart that I doubt that I shall ever achieve again, so I pray that you are in a quiet room as you hear these words. My secret is that I need God – that I am sick and can no longer make it alone. I need God to help me give, because I no longer seem to be capable of giving; to help me to be kind, as I no longer seem capable of kindness; to help me love as I seem beyond being able to love.[7]

Many others are conscious of the same need – they need God. But who is he? What is he like? David Lean, the film maker, has said: "I'm not a Quaker now. I don't know what I am. I don't think it's a godless universe, but I don't know what God is. We're still trying to find out what makes us tick - like plumbers trying to mend Swiss watches." Spike Milligan was asked, "Do you ever pray?" He replied, "Yes of course. Desperately – all the time – 'Get me out of this mess'. But I don't know who I am praying to."

Madonna was interviewed recently about her religious views:

Q: "When you gathered your dancers around you during the 'Blond Ambition' tour to pray before going on stage, who were you praying to?"

A: "Who was I praying to?" She repeats the question, stalling for time. "Everyone in the room and my idea of God."

Q: "Is there a god?"

A: "Yes", she replied quickly. "There's my god. Everyone has their own god."

Q: "Tell me about him."

A: "I can't describe it."

Q: "You have a good idea though?"

A: "Yes", the voice was strained, quiet. "To me, sometimes, I don't know if it's a being or more like the highest state of my consciousness, like trying to rise above everyday life and the things that bring you down, and mortality and things like that . . . It's like calling on any power I have inside myself. It's a protector, an adviser, it's soothing, comforting . . . and nonjudgmental."

Q: "But is it a supreme being?"

A: "I don't know. You know I really have unformed ideas about it because I could change my mind in about half an hour. I think religion should be a very personal thing. It's what you get your strength from."

Q: "So it's an inner matter rather than an organised religion?"

A: "Yeah, I think." By this time she was almost whispering.[8]

What is God like?

Madonna's religion fits very well into the spirit of the age. It is questioning and undogmatic. But it is also confused – there is no firm ground, no conviction. Is that confusion and uncertainty just a fact of life? Can we ever find out what God is like?

Imagine that I am in a room with some people who know nothing about me. I set them a question "What am I like?" Some might decide to guess: "I reckon that you are a policeman from Cleethorpes who enjoys ballroom dancing" or, "I like to think of you as an accountant from Balham with a dog called Rufus." They could go on like that for hours without getting any closer to the facts. And even if, by chance, they did get close, they would not know it. The wise ones would recognize that from the beginning and acknowledge their ignorance. But that would not be a reason to despair of ever finding an answer. The sensible approach would be to ask me to tell them what I amlike. And I could tell them the truth – that I am a vicar from Oxford with a strange passion for Hampshire County Cricket Club and very definitely no pets.

Now let us change the question: "What is God like?" If we cannot know about a fellow human being we have not met before, what hope have we got with God? He is way beyond us by definition. There is no way that our tiny minds can begin to approach certain knowledge about him. We can guess ("I like to think of God as an old man with a white bushy beard and twinkly eyes") but we would be foolish to give any authority to such speculations – we are just stabbing in the dark. But what if God was to take the initiative and make himself known to us? Then we could know the truth about him with certainty. The only way that we can know what God is like is if he takes the initiative and tells us. The Bible claims to be a record of him doing just that. From beginning to end it shows God taking the initiative, revealing his character to people and calling on them to live in love and obedience to him. It is not about the human quest for God – as we saw in the last chapter, our nature is to run away from him. Biblical religion does not begin on earth with human beings reaching out for the divine. No – it begins in heaven with God in his great love deciding to make himself known. It is "revelation" from him.

There is space here for only a very brief summary of the contents of the Bible. For the rest of this chapter we will consider the Old Testament, which is concerned with the time before Jesus. God revealed himself to the people of Israel through his actions and his explanation of them. Our quick survey of the main events, or turning points, will therefore teach us about what God is like.

1: *The loving God*

Amazingly, despite the way we disobey and ignore him, God still wants us to know him. We could hardly complain if the Bible ended at Genesis chapter 3 with the account of the Fall. Why should God bother with us after that? But the fact that there are another sixty-six books to follow speaks loudly of the great truth that God is loving and merciful – he has not given up on us.

It all started with a promise. God appeared to Abraham, a man who lived near the Persian Gulf roughly 4000 years ago.[9] In effect, God promised Abraham that he would reverse the effects of his judgement after the Fall. Abraham's descendants would become a great nation who would be given a land to live in. Although all human beings deserved to remain separated from him, God declared his intention of calling back to himself people who could then enjoy the benefits of his friendship once more. It would consist initially of Abraham's descendants, the Jews, but from the start God's promise made it clear that people from all nations would one day be included. The Bible records how that promise was gradually fulfilled.

It all seemed a very long way off in the beginning. Abraham's wife Sarah was barren and was long past the menopause. How could a great nation descend from him if he could not produce any children? But God always does what he promises to do and a miracle happened: Sarah gave birth to a son, Isaac. Gradually the family grew as the generations passed, but they were still far from being a great nation and they had very little land that they could call their own – certainly not the great land that God had promised Abraham.. But God was faithful. He continued to protect them, even preserving them at the time of a famine that threatened to wipe them out. The same care and concern was shown to them throughout their history.

Why? It's a question we are bound to ask. Why did God choose the Jews to be his people and not some other nation? He gave his own answer through the prophet Moses, who spoke to the Israelites and said: "The LORD your God has chosen you out of all the peoples on the face of the earth to be his people, his treasured possession. The LORD did not set his affection on you because you were more numerous than other peoples, for you were the fewest of all the peoples. But it was because the LORD loved you . . ."[10] There was nothing in the Jews that warranted God's favour – all human beings since the Fall deserve nothing but his anger. God chose them simply out of love. He did not have to care for them – he could have wiped his hands of them and the rest of us. The fact that he did not reveals him to be a God of amazing love.

A common misconception is to view God as a Shylock who will only give to us once we have first given him our pound of flesh. He waits to see evidence of our commitment to him before he will do anything for us. Nothing could be further from the truth. Abraham had done nothing to deserve the wonderful promises he received and that crucial place in God's plan for the world. The Jews did nothing to deserve their status as the people of God. And we do not deserve the food we eat, the clothes we wear or anything else we enjoy in this world.

One Christmas my father bought two state-of-the-art squash rackets. He kept one for himself and gave the other to me. We were soon on the court trying them out. The game did not go according to plan as far as I was concerned and in my frustration I smashed the racket against the wall. I regretted it as soon as I had done it, but the damage had been done – there was a crack right through the frame. I deserved a strong ticking off, but my father said nothing. He just went to the changing room, fetched his old racket, which should have been retired years before, and carried on playing with that. He insisted that I played with his new one and would not have it back at the end. That is love – undeserved love. It is a weak illustration of the kind of love that God shows to us again and again. We deserve nothing from God except his anger. But despite the fact that we live in his world as if he does not exist and disobey him again and again, he still does not destroy us. Instead he continues to shower us with good things. He has not given up on his world. His promises to Abraham reveal his determination to call a people to himself and to reveal his love to them – he is a loving God.

2: *The mighty God*

The Old Testament reveals God to be not just loving but also mighty. He has the power to fulfil his loving plans for his people. That was not easy. By the start of Exodus, the second book of the Bible, we find the Israelites as slaves to the Egyptians, a long way from home. The great promises God had made to Abraham must have seemed like a sick joke. They had been told that they were to be a great nation blessed by God with their own land to live in, yet here they were as slaves in a foreign land. But God had not forgotten his promises. He still loved them and was determined to rescue them. He raised up Moses to lead them. Moses went to Pharaoh to ask for his people's freedom. When this was denied, God inflicted a series of plagues on the Egyptians. The final one proved conclusive: the plague on the firstborn, the first "Passover". God announced his intention to pass through the land of Egypt in judgement. The first-born sons in every family would be killed. That would include the Israelites' children – they had disobeyed God as much as the Egyptians. But God wanted to save the Israelites, so he provided a way of escape for them. Each family was to kill a lamb instead of their son and to daub its blood on the door of their house. When God saw the blood he would "pass over" that house and not bring judgement.

Imagine the scene in a Jewish house. The eldest son, Samuel, has just gone to bed. His parents have told him that God is going to kill the firstborn sons in Egypt that night, but that he will be safe because a lamb will be killed instead. Do you think he would have slept? It would not have been long before he was downstairs: "Dad, have you done it yet?" "Don't worry Sam, I'll do it," his father replies. After a few more minutes of toss-ing and turning, he would have been down again: "Dad, have you done it?" "Not yet. I'll do it straight after the news." Another twenty minutes later and he would be down once more: "Dad . . ."And then his father would have shown him the blood on the door which proved that the lamb had died, and at last he could have gone to sleep, confident that he was safe. That episode taught an important lesson. God rescues by providing a stand-in. His people deserve to be punished for their disobedience, but in his love God provides a substitute to take what they deserve in their place so that they can be forgiven and enjoy friendship with God.

It happened just as God had said it would. The Israelites were spared because they killed the passover lambs, but the firstborn Egyptians all died. At last Pharaoh let the Israelites go. But he soon changed his mind and sent his army to chase after them. There seemed no hope for them against such powerful opponents, but God intervened again. When they reached the Red Sea the water was miraculously parted for them and they walked through it. But as the Egyptians went through, the water returned and they were destroyed. God had rescued his people by inflicting an humiliating defeat on the most powerful nation of the day. The Israelites could hardly take the credit – from the start they had simply been witnesses to God's mighty power.

After the "exodus" from Egypt the next objective was to enter the land of Canaan, or Palestine, which God had promised them at the time of Abraham. This was achieved under Joshua, Moses' successor, through a series of victories against the inhabitants of that land. In the years that followed God continued to preserve them in the face of opposition from foreign nations and they began to gain a secure hold over the promised land. He instituted a monarchy for them and, under the great kings David and his son Solomon, they reached the high point of their history. God's promises to Abraham had been fulfilled, at least in part. They were a great nation, living in their own land and enjoying the blessing of their God.

All that had been achieved by God – the mighty God. Every tribe and nation at that time had its own god or gods. But the Israelites were unique – they claimed to follow the one true God, the creator of everything; all the others were lifeless idols. It was quite a claim. They began as an insignificant tribe and then became a fairly minor nation and yet, they insisted, their God was the God who had made the universe and was in complete control of everything. His victories on behalf of his people proved to them that their faith was built on solid ground – God had shown himself to be more powerful than any human power. Nothing could stand in the way of him fulfilling his purposes. One of their prophets, Isaiah, expressed it powerfully:

> Do you not know? Have you not heard? . . . He sits enthroned above the circle of the earth, and its people are like grasshoppers. He stretches out the heavens like a canopy, and spreads them out like a tent to live in. He brings princes to naught and reduces the rulers of this world to nothing. No sooner are they planted, no sooner are they sown, no sooner do they take root in the ground, than he blows on them and they wither, and a whirlwind sweeps them away like chaff. "To whom will you compare me? Or who is my equal?" says the Holy One. Lift your eyes and look to the heavens: Who created all these? He who brings out the starry host one by one and calls them each by name. Because of his great power and mighty strength, not one of them is missing.[12]

3: The holy God

I am not much of a gardener, but I happened to be listening to *Gardener's Question Time* on the radio one day. The final question for the panel was: "Who would you most like to entertain for tea in your garden and why?" One expert replied: "God - I've got a few questions I should like to ask him, like why he made greenfly and what moles were created for." Then he added, "It would be quite entertaining." I was very struck by those last few words. It is true that God is a loving God, but the Bible makes it clear that there is nothing "entertaining" about him. He is a God who is not comfortable but awesome or, to use the Bible's word, "holy". He is set so far above us in his perfection that there can be no easy familiarity with him.

Soon after God had rescued the Israelites from Egypt he met with them at Mount Sinai where he told them how he wanted them to live as his people. The law that he revealed to them there through Moses revealed his standards. They are summarized in the Ten Commandments.[13]

There appears to be a moral vacuum in our society, perhaps especially amongst the young. For the past forty years or so, the old traditional values have been overturned in the name of personal freedom. The individual must have the right, within a few limited constraints, to do exactly what he or she wants. This new age, the "permissive society", was heralded with a fanfare in the 1960s, but the band plays no more. The dream has become a nightmare as we begin to reap what we have sown: an accelerating crime rate, the disintegration of family life and a lack of respect for authority. It is no wonder that many are realizing that the rejection of the old values was a great mistake. It was because he sensed that mood that John Major launched his ill-fated "Back to Basics" campaign in 1993. It failed, not just because some Conservative politicians showed themselves incapable of living up to the standards they set. There was a more fundamental problem: just what should the "basics" be? There is no moral consensus any more. Once we reject God we can have no firm foundation. Morality becomes just a matter of opinion, which changes with cultural context and individual preference. In the long run that leaves an uncomfortable choice between moral anarchy or rules imposed by a dictatorial state.

But it need not be like that. Morality is not just a social construct; it is rooted in the eternal character of God himself. The Ten Commandments reflect that character. God is faithful, so he calls on us to be the same: "You shall not commit adultery". He is truthful, so we are not to lie. He is generous, so we should not steal or covet. He is the basis of the moral standards revealed in his law.

We can summarize his character in one word: "Holy". The holiness of God is the "Godness" of God. It is what sets him apart from everyone else – his moral perfection. He is the God of absolute goodness. In the law he calls on his people to reflect that holiness in their own lives.

But, of course, they cannot do it – not perfectly. That creates a problem. How can the holy God live amongst a sinful people without compromising his perfection? That problem became acute when God symbolically came to live with the Israelites in the "Tabernacle", a tent which travelled around with them in the wilderness before they entered the land of Canaan. It remained a problem after they entered the land and God's presence was focused in a permanent structure – the magnificent Temple in Jerusalem.

One of my great heroes as a boy was Bobby Moore, who was the captain of the England football team that won the World Cup in 1966. I think I probably saw the match but I cannot claim to remember it – I was only one at the time. Shortly before Moore died of cancer a few years ago, he was asked what it felt like to go up to the balcony to receive the Jules Rimet trophy from Her Majesty the Queen. "It must have been a wonderful experience to do that in front of a home crowd," said the interviewer. But he replied, "No, it was terrifying, because as I was going up the steps to the balcony I saw that the Queen was wearing some beautiful white gloves. I looked at my hands and realised that they were covered in Wembley mud, and I thought 'How can I shake hands with her like this? – I'll make her gloves dirty.' " I have seen the footage a number of times since then. As Bobby Moore walks up the steps he can be seen desperately wiping his hands against his shorts to try to get them clean. If he is worried about approaching the Queen with his muddy hands and her white gloves, how much more worried should we be. God does not just have white hands; he is perfectly white all over - the holy God. And we do not just have dirty hands; we are dirty everywhere and deep within.

Much of the law revealed to Moses is concerned with the solution God provided to this problem. God set apart priests who were to perform sacrifices on behalf of the people. An individual Israelite, guilty of wrong-doing as we all are, deserved to die as he approached the holy God in his Temple. But God allowed an animal to be killed instead, just as he had done at the first Passover. As a result, God's anger against his sin was turned away and he was forgiven. These sacrifices, performed year after year, were designed to teach some important lessons. They showed that God was a holy God who was set apart from his creation in his perfection and could not be approached lightly – we all deserve to die in his presence. And yet the sacrifices also revealed that there was hope. It was possible to come near to him as a substitute was killed in the place of his people.

4: The just God

As time passed, the Israelites became complacent.
God had looked after them for so long despite their
sin that they presumed he would continue to do so, no
matter how they behaved. God raised up some
prophets to warn them against such presumption. It
was true that they had been protected in the past so
that they had become a great nation, but they could
not be sure that that would continue. They should
have realized that when civil war broke out after the
death of Solomon and the kingdom split in two. The
glory days had ended, but still the people were confident that all would be well. It was at this time that
God's word came to them through great men like
Jeremiah, Ezekiel and Isaiah. The warning was clear:
if they did not repent and return to their God, he
would punish them and evict them from the land that
he had given them. The disobedience continued and,
in time, God's patience ran out. Judgement came
and culminated in the defeat of the Jews by the
Babylonians. They destroyed Jerusalem and its
Temple and then took its people into exile. Judgement
had come. The Israelites had learnt that God was no
soft touch. They knew from their history that he was
a loving God who looked after them despite their
wickedness, but that did not mean that he condoned
it. He is a God of justice who must punish wrongdoing.

It is not fashionable to believe in a God who gets
angry and judges. If we believe in him at all we tend
to imagine a kindly old man who is always smiling at
us – Ronnie Barker with a big white beard. But a
moment's thought will show us how dreadful it
would be to believe in such a God. Do we really want

a God like that – one who smiles at us no matter what we do? Imagine him welcoming some of the great tyrants into his heaven with these words: "Adolf, how good to see you! It doesn't matter that you have been responsible for the death of six million Jews and untold misery throughout the world. Come in!" Or what about the drug addict who mugs an old woman and leaves her dead just so that he can get a few pounds for the next fix? Would you want to worship a God who was unmoved by that – a God who carried on smiling?

In one telling moment in the Inspector Morse series Lewis turns to his boss and asks, "What do you think about God and that?" Morse replies: "I think there are times when I wish to God there was one – a God who dispenses justice. I'd like to believe in that." The Bible insists that there is such a God. He is a God of justice, of blazing "holiness". He loves what is right and hates what is evil, and gets angry when he sees it. He does not just turn a blind eye. Justice demands that wrongdoing is punished. That is good news. We do not live in an amoral universe governed by an indifferent God. But the flip side, of course, is that he must punish us when we do what is wrong.

The exile of the Jews of Babylon was a devastating blow to the Israelites. Some did return after a few years, but never again did the Israelites return to the heights they had enjoyed under the great kings David and Solomon. From then on they were a weak nation dominated by other powers. They had no kings of their own and although a temple was built, it was nothing like the great one constructed by Solomon. The awful experience of the exile and its aftermath underlined what God had long said through the prophets. The promises he had made to Abraham all those years before would not be completely fulfilled in the nation of Israel.

5: The faithful God

The prophets did not just bring a message of judgement from God; they also spoke of hope. God had promised Abraham that he would bless his offspring and so bring blessing to people of all nations, and he was determined to keep that promise – he is a faithful God. Fulfilment would only come with the arrival of God's "Messiah". Only then would people of all nations fully be able to know God and enjoy the blessings of a friendship with him.

The prophets spoke of good times ahead in terms of action replay. "Do you remember the beautiful land we lived in, the great King David who ruled over us, and that magnificent Temple Solomon built? In the age to come it will be like that again, only better." There would be a new king, a new temple, a new Jerusalem. The great nation of Israel that God established was, at its high point under David and Solomon, a model of what he would do in the future on a far larger scale. God would act not just to restore the fortunes of one racial group; he would also put the whole world right and undo all the effects of the Fall. There would be a new creation: "Behold, I will create new heavens and a new earth. The former things will not be remembered, nor will they come to mind."[14] And the great event that would pull the trigger to start this great transformation was the coming of the Messiah:

> For to us a child is born,
> > to us a son is given,
> > and the government will be on his shoulders.

And he will be called
  Wonderful Counsellor, Mighty God,
  Everlasting Father, Prince of Peace.
Of the increase of his government and peace
  there will be no end.
He will reign on David's throne
  and over his kingdom,
establishing and upholding it with justice and
  righteousness
  from that time on and for ever.
The zeal of the LORD Almighty will accomplish this.[15]

Here is my servant, whom I uphold,
  my chosen one in whom I delight;
I will put my Spirit on him
  and he will bring justice to the nations.
He will not shout or cry out,
  or raise his voice in the streets.
A bruised reed he will not break
  and a smouldering wick he will not snuff out.
In faithfulness he will bring forth justice;
  he will not falter or be discouraged
till he establishes justice on earth.
  In his law the islands will put their hope.[16]

He was despised and rejected by men,
  a man of sorrows, and familiar with suffering.
Like one from whom men hide their faces
  he was despised, and we esteemed him not.
Surely he took up our infirmities
  and carried our sorrows,
yet we considered him stricken by God,
  smitten by him, and afflicted.
But he was pierced for our transgressions,
  he was crushed for our iniquities;

the punishment that brought us peace was upon him,
    and by his wounds we are healed.
We all, like sheep, have gone astray,
    each of us has turned to his own way;
and the LORD has laid on him
    the iniquity of us all.
He was oppressed and afflicted,
    yet he did not open his mouth;
he was led like a lamb to the slaughter,
    and as a sheep before her shearers is silent,
    so he did not open his mouth.[17]

That is where the Old Testament ends – waiting; waiting for one to be born. He would come as a strange mixture – the "mighty God" who rules over all and establishes an eternal reign of peace and justice, and yet also a suffering servant, despised and rejected by men.

So there is the first stage of the revelation of God about himself. God reveals himself to us through his actions towards his ancient people and his explanation of those actions in the Bible. When set the question, "What is God like?", we are not left to our own guesses like Madonna's; instead, we can give a confident answer because he has made himself known.

But how can we be sure that the Bible really is God's revelation? Many other religions claim revelation from him. How can we be so confident that they are wrong and the Bible is right? And isn't that an arrogant claim anyway in today's pluralistic society? Those are questions which will be addressed in the next chapter. The answer is bound up with the coming of the one who was promised. Could Jesus of Nazareth really have been the great Messiah? If so, he is at the centre of God's plans for the world and for your life, both now and for eternity.

<u>A History of the World</u>

The story so far:

1) Creation

2) The Fall

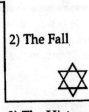

3) The History of Israel

Notes

1. Jan Morris, *Oxford* (OUP, 1978), 180.
2. *The Penguin Book of English Verse* (Penguin, 1956), 344.
3. Ted Harrison, *Diana: Icon and Sacrifice* (Lion, 1998).
4. Melanie Philipps, quoted in Nick Pollard, *Why Do They Do That?* (Lion, 1998), 81.
5. *The Times*, September 1997.
6. Douglas Coupland, *Life After God* (Touchstone, 1994).
7. Coupland, *Life After God*, 359.
8. Interview with Andrew Neil in *The Sunday Times*.
9. Genesis 12:1–7.
10. Deuteronomy 7:6–7.
11. The sea of reeds.
12. Isaiah 40:21–26.
13. Exodus 20:1–17.
14. Isaiah 65:17.
15. Isaiah 9:6–7.
16. Isaiah 42:1–4.
17. Isaiah 53:3–7.

4

The Down-To-Earth God

Can we believe in 'capital T' Truth any more?

All I said was, "The Christian Union is holding a series of meetings this week and I was wondering if you would be interested in coming along to one of them." But Sanjay was furious. He was not a close friend but we had often chatted in the hall where we both lived as students and we got on well. This time was different. As soon as I had given the invitation, he told me to sit down on a chair in his room and began to lecture me. How dare I invite him to a Christian meeting? Did I think that his Sikh religion was not good enough? What arrogance! What a nerve!

In a recent poll 66 per cent of Americans said they believed there was no such thing as absolute truth. The percentage was even higher amongst young adults between the ages of eighteen and twenty-five – 72 per cent.[1] According to the predominant view in our culture it is still possible to say that some things are true and others are false. "Two plus two equals four" is a true statement. "The boiling temperature of water is one degree Celsius" is a false statement. The one who says "that is a matter of opinion" is rightly regarded as a fool. In the so-called "public world of facts", scientific methodology can discover "the truth". But the common assumption is that truth is not an appropriate category for the "private world of values" – the world of religion and morality. We cannot scientifically prove that Christianity is right and other religions are wrong or that monogamy is right and promiscuity is wrong. Such matters belong to the realm of opinion. We are entitled to our own beliefs in these areas, but we must not imply that we are right and others are wrong – that is to break one of the few fundamental moral rules left in our society: "Thou shalt be tolerant". It was because he judged that I had transgressed that law that Sanjay was so angry.

"Tolerance", in its modern sense, means more than accepting the right of others to a different point of view. According to the common contemporary understanding, it also means accepting the possibility that they might be right and that I might be wrong. If we are allowed to use the word "truth" at all in the sphere of morality and belief it is to speak of "what is true for me", with the "tolerant" implication that "what is true for you" may be very different.

Lynne Franks has written about her religious quest: "In June 1992 I started a four-year journey to search for the truth. I found that there are many self-proclaimed prophets and I realised that much discrimination needs to go into the selection of your spiritual path . . . I'm just a woman *on her own journey to her truth.*"[2] Those last few words are very striking. She is not seeking to discover *the* truth, but rather *her* truth. Jane Turney described a similar approach in an article headed "I believe in pick 'n' mix spirituality":

I am one of a growing number of people who feel we can no longer rely on external authority to run our lives safely – we feel let down by orthodox religions, scientists, politicians, doctors and economists, and think that we have to look for our own answers. This may mean that I visit an astrologer, a Buddhist meditation teacher, and a Christian mystic as part of my search. It does not necessarily mean that I am looking for a quick fix, rather that I recognise that there are many roads to God, and that ultimately I am the only person responsible for my journey home.[3]

In a "pick 'n' mix" world the consumer is king. A recent Sainsbury's advert proudly proclaimed: "We sell 37 types of fish on our fresh fish counters – including tuna, sea bass and tilapia from Jamaica. Fancy a fresh kind of sausage? We have 40. We sell 103 cheeses from 13 countries. Over the year, choose from 35 varieties of apples." That is the world we live in – a world full of choices. It would be ridiculous for you to insist that there is only one cheese worthy of the name from the 103 on offer in Sainsbury's and to demand that everyone else follow your example and stick with Cheddar and only Cheddar. How dare you impose your choice on the rest of us and imply that you are the sole arbiter of what makes a good cheese? That is the height of arrogance. Are not those who make similar claims for their religion equally guilty? That is the objection that many have against Christianity. It is arrogant – it claims to have the truth, which is offensive to all those who believe something different.

Here is how one writer has described the so-called "postmodern" mindset: "Truth is what you find for yourself, not what someone imposes on you . . . It no longer says 'Here is the truth – believe it!' It says – 'Try this for size' ".[4] Jean-François Lyotard defined postmodernism as "an incredulity towards meta-narratives".[5] There are no all-embracing answers to the big questions of life – just questions. It sounds so attractive doesn't it? Surely we would be better off if we abandoned any arrogant claim to exclusive truth and recognized that such a concept is just a fantasy? It does not exist; and even if it does, we can never be sure we have found it.

But would we? Would we be better off? Think of the consequences. If truth is just a fantasy then life has no meaning. We are adrift in a sea of relativity with no anchor to secure us – nothing to make sense of it all. The modern understanding of "tolerance" sounds so attractive at first, but is it? D.L. Sayers, the novelist, summed it up well: "In the world it is called 'Tolerance', but in hell it is called 'Despair' . . . the sin that believes in nothing, cares for nothing, enjoys nothing, lives for nothing, and remains alive because there is nothing for which it will die." That is where relativism leads us. It has bred a generation which has nothing to live for, and nothing to die for either. It may be that we are forced to that position. If the facts as we see them drive us to the conclusion that there is no truth then there is no merit in shutting our minds and believing something else just because it is more palatable. But given that the nihilism of today is so profoundly depressing, surely we would be wise not to embrace it before we have convinced ourselves that the assumption behind it is right: that we cannot discover "the truth" with any certainty. We Christians want to insist with Scully and Mulder that "the truth is out there" and that we do not have to look very far to find it, because it has come looking for us. And that truth is not some deep philosophical theory – it is a person, Jesus of Nazareth.

That brings us back to where we left off at the end of the last chapter. I argued there that we can know about God because he has revealed himself to us. As we have seen, the Old Testament of the Bible claims to be revelation from him, showing him to be a loving, holy, mighty, just and faithful God. It is not just one human attempt among many to describe what God might be like; it is the truth.

Such language does not fit comfortably in our modern world – it is too definite, too exclusive. Mahatma Gandhi expressed the feelings of many when he said, "The soul of religions is one, but it is encased in a multitude of forms. Truth is the property of no single scripture . . . I cannot ascribe exclusive divinity to Jesus. He is as divine as Krishna or Rama or Mohammed or Zoroaster."[6] It sounds appealing – to say that there need be no disagreement because all religions are basically saying the same thing; they are just different paths up the same mountain. But it does not require much knowledge of the different religions to know that that cannot be right. Of course they are similar at points, but there are also some fundamental disagreements. Is there just one God, as Christianity and Islam teach, or many gods, as Hindus believe? Is he the eternal creator or an ephemeral illusion – according to the Buddhist nothing really exists. Are we accepted by him on the basis of our faith in Christ or our good deeds? The philosopher Bertrand Russell was surely right when he said, "It is evident as a matter of logic that since they [the great religions of the world] disagree, not more than one of them can be true."[7] They could all be wrong, but they cannot all be right. Which still leaves the question: Why believe this one? How can you be so sure that the Bible's claim to revelation is right while the others are wrong? The answer is: Because of Jesus. Everything hinges on him.

Who is Jesus?

The birth of Jesus is the next great "turning point" in the history of the world. It was a humble start to life: he was born 2000 years ago in a manger in Bethlehem amongst the animals in a stable. The Christmas cards glamorize the scene. Mary looks remarkably healthy for a woman who has just given birth; the baby Jesus has a gentle smile ("no crying he makes", as the carol "Away in a Manger" puts it); even the straw looks as if it has been washed, rinsed and tumble-dried. The reality would have been rather different: dirty and smelly. There was very little to suggest that this boy was anything out of the ordinary. In one sense he was not – he was fully human. Yet the Christian claim is that he was also fully divine, God himself in human form – the down-to-earth God. Colonel James Irwin was one of the first men to walk on the moon. Soon after that experience he said these words: "The greatest miracle is not that man stood on the moon. It is that God came and stood on earth."

What do you make of Jesus? Most people today have hardly given him a thought. That was certainly true of me. I had a vague idea of a rather weak figure – "gentle Jesus meek and mild", who went around being nice to everyone. He had long permed hair, Clarks sandals and a permanent smile – fine for those who like that kind of thing, but not really my cup of tea. It was then that I was challenged to read one of the Gospel accounts of his life in the Bible. I had read bits of it before, but never as an adult. It completely changed my view of Jesus. Here was a man I could not ignore – he was so compelling, powerful and real. He was a man like no other. Christianity is the truth because Jesus is the truth. It is unique because he is unique.

The uniqueness of his claims

Chris Eubank, the boxer, must be one of the most accomplished self-publicists of his generation. He said recently: "I have no vices. I am a hero. Go and look it up in the dictionary and you will find a picture of me."[8] There is a man who does not have a problem with low self-esteem! But that is nothing compared to some of the things that Jesus said about himself. We find in him a remarkable combination. He was a humble man, everyone agrees on that, and yet he made some extraordinary egocentric claims.

In his first recorded words in Mark's account of his life in the New Testament he says: "The time has come. The kingdom of God is near. Repent and believe the good news."[9] There is no doubt what he was saying. The Jews had been waiting for generations for the fulfilment of the great promises God had made in the Old Testament. Ever since the Fall, human beings had rejected God's rule and the world was spoilt as a result. But the prophets had foretold a time when the Messiah would come to re-establish the kingdom of God and put things right again. He would be a great ruler ("Wonderful Counsellor, Mighty God,"[10]) and a suffering servant ("despised and rejected by men"[11]). And Jesus was saying, "the moment you have all been waiting for has arrived. I am the one to whom the prophets pointed, the one who will bring about the fulfilment of all God's loving promises." On one occasion in a synagogue he read a prophecy from the book of Isaiah which spoke of the coming Messiah. As he sat down he said: "Today this scripture is fulfilled in your hearing."[12] Speaking of the whole of the Old Testament he said: "These are the scriptures that testify about me."[13] The kingdom of God was near because God was near. At last he had done what he had promised to do and visited his world in the person of his Son.

Most religious leaders point away from themselves. "Do you want to find God?" they ask. "Go to that holy place" or "Read that holy book". But Jesus said "Come to me!"[14] "I am the way, the truth and the life. No-one comes to the Father except through me".[15] "Anyone who has seen me has seen the Father".[16] "I and the Father are one".[17] He even claimed to forgive the sins of those he had never met before. The Jewish religious leaders saw the implications of that claim and were horrified: "Why does this fellow talk like that? He's blaspheming! Who can forgive sins but God alone?"[18] Don't take it from me. Get hold of a Gospel in modern English and read it for yourself. "Mark" is the shortest – it will only take you a couple of hours. If you dare, you could start by saying a prayer like this: "God, if you are there, please help me to know the truth about Jesus Christ."

As I continued to read from the Gospels I realized that Jesus simply did not fit the category that I had previously placed him in. I had always assumed that he was a good man, on a par with many of the other great religious teachers in history. But I soon discovered that he was very different from those other men. C.S. Lewis, the author of the Narnia books, put it well in an essay entitled "What are we to make of Jesus Christ?":

> If you had gone to Buddha and asked him, 'Are you the son of Bramah?' he would have said, 'My son, you are in the vale of illusion.' If you had gone to Socrates and asked 'Are you the son of Zeus?' he would have laughed at you. If you had gone to Mohammed and asked 'Are you Allah?' he would first have rent his clothes and then cut your head off. If you had asked Confucius 'Are you heaven?' he would probably have replied, 'Remarks which are not in accordance with nature are in bad taste.'[19]

Jesus made unique claims. He cannot be placed alongside these men as simply one good man amongst a number of great religious teachers – his claims about himself do not allow that option. Jesus' contemporaries certainly recognized that. "He was never regarded as a mere moral teacher. He did not produce that effect on any of the people who actually met him. He produced mainly three effects: hatred, terror, adoration. There was no trace of people expressing mild approval."[20] A man who claimed to be God could not be "just a good man". He was either much less, a fraud or a lunatic, or much more – the one he claimed to be, God himself in human form. The journalist Malcolm Muggeridge saw the implications soon after he began to investigate the Christian faith. He wrote later in his autobiography: "I understood that Jesus could not be turned into just a great man without diminishing him to the point that Christianity became too trivial to be taken seriously. He was God or he was nothing."

But all this assumes that Jesus actually made these claims about himself. The New Testament writers say that he did, but could they not have been wrong? How can we be sure that the Jesus of the Gospels is the same as the Jesus of history? Writers such as A.N. Wilson are convinced that he is not. In an interview at the time of the publication of a recent book of his about Jesus he said: "His rage at the activities of the money-changers in the temple would have been as nothing to his rage at the activities of the Christians who made him into a god."[21]

So did the writers of the New Testament put the great divine claims of Jesus into his mouth or did he really say them? To what extent can we be sure that the Gospels are history rather than legend? If you want a fuller examination of these issues you should read F.F. Bruce: *Are the New Testament Documents Reliable?* or Paul Barnett: *Is the New Testament History?*[22] There is only room here to consider briefly a number of points that are sometimes made:

1: The Gospels are just a collection of myths

- There is no doubt about the historical existence of Jesus. The Roman historians Pliny the Younger (AD 61–114), Tacitus (AD 55–118) and Suetonius (AD 69–140) all refer to him, as does Josephus, the non-Christian Jew, writing in AD 93. Between them they refer to the fact that his followers worshipped him as God and called him the Messiah and that he was executed in Judaea when Pontius Pilate was Governor.

- The Gospels were based on eye-witness accounts. Matthew and John were among Jesus' first disciples. They had lived with him for the three years of his active ministry. John stressed in one of his letters in the New Testament that he knew what he was talking about when he wrote about Jesus: "That which was from the beginning, which we have *seen with our eyes*, which we have looked at and our hands have touched – this we proclaim".[23] The early Christian writer Papias, writing in AD 140, tells us that Mark relied on the apostle Peter for his information. That same Peter wrote in one of his letters: "We did not follow cleverly invented stories when we told you about the power and coming of the Lord Jesus Christ, but we were *eyewitnesses* of his majesty." [24] The other Gospel writer, Luke, also took pains to ensure that he got his facts right. It is clear from his opening words that he wants to be taken seriously as an historian. He was not simply recording legends; he assured Theophilus, to whom the book was addressed, that he wrote the truth:

> Many have undertaken to draw up an account of the things that have been fulfilled among us, just as they were handed down to us by those who from the first were *eyewitnesses* and servants of the word. Therefore, since I myself have carefully investigated everything from the beginning, it seemed good also to me to write an orderly account for you, most excellent Theophilus, so that you might know the certainty of the things that you have been taught.[25]

- The first Gospels were probably written only about 30 years after Jesus' death, during the lifetime of many who saw and heard him. If they had got important details wrong there would have been plenty of early Christians ready to disagree. But there is no record that any of the disciples questioned the authenticity of the Gospel accounts. From the start they were accepted as reliable.

2: The authors were biased

- It is true that the writers of the Gospels were all Christians and therefore wrote from a particular standpoint. But that is true of any historian. The question to ask is not "Were they biased?" but rather "Did the fact that they were followers of Jesus influence them to write what was not true?" There is absolutely no evidence that it did. Many historical references in the New Testament have been verified by other writings and archaeological discoveries. For example, Luke, who wrote both "Luke" and "Acts" in the New Testament, included in his account a great many geographical and political details which have been proved accurate over and over again.

- If they had invented much of what they wrote, why were they willing to suffer for it so much? Most of the first apostles died for their faith.

3: We cannot trust such ancient documents

- All the evidence shows that the Gospels we have now are almost exactly as they were when they were first written. We have many ancient manuscripts of the Gospels. The earliest fragment is the "John Rylands papyrus" which contains a section of John's Gospel and dates from AD 130, only a few decades after it was written. There are about 5000 Greek manuscript copies of the complete text of the Gospels, all of which were produced before AD 350. There are remarkably few differences between them, none of which concern a matter of any significance. Compare that with other ancient histories. The oldest manuscripts of Tacitus, Caesar and Thucydides come 800, 850 and 1300 years after the originals. Yet scholars accept these single manuscripts as reliable historical documents. The former Cambridge theologian John Robinson concludes: "the wealth of manuscripts, and above all the narrow interval of time between the writing and the earliest extant copies, make it [the New Testament] by far the best attested text of any ancient writing in the world."[26]

I am convinced that the New Testament documents can be relied upon to give us an accurate historical account of the real Jesus. He really did say the things that are reported as spoken by him in the Gospels. We must now consider the evidence they give us to support his claim to be not just one amongst many religious teachers, but rather the Messiah, the Son of God himself. He not only made unique claims; he also lived a unique life.

The uniqueness of his life

A few years ago David Icke, a former television sports reporter, shocked the nation when he announced that he was the son of God. We did not all fall on our knees in worship. Such an extraordinary claim demands strong evidence to support it if it is to be taken seriously, and Icke produced none. So what of Jesus?

Having rejected my old opinion that Jesus was just a good man I looked for other possible explanations as I kept reading the Gospels. Could he not have been deluded, like many other Messianic pretenders over the years? But that just did not fit the facts. The Jesus of whom I read was the sanest man there could ever be. No one else has taught like him. Many have found that as they have read his words he seems to be speaking directly to them; it is as if he understands them inside out. His words in the Sermon on the Mount are universally acknowledged to be among the wisest ever spoken: "Blessed are the poor in spirit, for theirs is the kingdom of heaven." "You have heard that it was said 'Love your neighbour and hate your enemy'. But I tell you: Love your enemies and pray for those who persecute you." "Do not judge or you too will be judged".[27] Are these the words of a madman?

Could he have been an evil man, knowing perfectly well that he was not the Son of God, but consciously deceiving people in order to get a following and make a name for himself? But again that did not fit the facts. I had never come across anyone so manifestly good. Love just poured out of him – to young and old, rich and poor, male and female – he loved everyone. And there was never a hint that he was out to feather his own nest. At the height of his popularity as a guru, Bhagwan Shree Rajneesh had 93 Rolls Royces and a private army equipped with assault rifles and riot guns. When finally arrested by US marshals, he was wearing 35 platinum and gold watches.[28] How different from Jesus. He had no home, no possessions to speak of and he ended his life in his early thirties on a Roman cross, leaving just a handful of committed followers behind him. If he had really been in it for personal gain he could surely have done better than that. At the very least he could have avoided execution. The charge that was brought against him was one of blasphemy – that he had claimed to be the Son of God. All he had to do was deny it and he would probably have escaped with a beating. But when asked by the high priest if he was "the Christ, the Son of God," he replied, "Yes, it is as you say".[29] Would he really have died for what he knew to be a lie? It just did not make sense.

Jesus' life and teaching supported the claims he made about himself. And then there were the miracles. He always refused to do miracles at the demand of the thrill-seekers who came to see him, but on occasions he did point to the miracles to support what he said about himself. John the Baptist was recognized by many as a great prophet from God. He taught that the Messiah was coming soon and urged his hearers to get ready for his arrival. He was arrested and put in prison and it was from there that he sent some of his followers to ask Jesus to confirm that he really was the one they had been waiting for. Jesus replied: "Go back and tell John what you hear and see: The blind receive sight, the lame walk, those who have leprosy are cured. The deaf hear, the dead are raised."[30] That was enough to satisfy John. The prophets had taught that such things would happen when the kingdom of God came. The Messiah would appear and defeat all the enemies that have spoiled life since the Fall and re-establish the reign of God. Jesus showed that he was the Messiah by proving that he had power over all the forces that no mere human could control. With a word he gave sight to the blind, healed the sick and raised the dead. Now, at last, God's kingdom was appearing on earth. The enemies of sickness, evil and death were forced to retreat when faced with the mighty power of God himself in his Son Jesus.

But can we really believe in such miracles today? It is worth noting that everyone acknowledged that Jesus was able to do such things – even his enemies could not deny them. The New Testament shows the Pharisees explaining them as the work of the devil.[31] There are references to the miracles in the writings of the non-Christian authors Josephus, in the first century, and Celsus in the second.[32] In both cases they are accepted as facts.

But were people then not more disposed to believe in such things in their pre-scientific age? We know more about the laws of nature and, as a result, our powers of credulity are kept within more realistic and rational bounds. That may be true, but we would be wise to heed the warning of C.S. Lewis:

> Suppose you put 5p into a drawer today, and 5p into the same drawer tomorrow. Do the laws of nature make it certain you'll find 10p there the day after? Of course – provided no one has been tampering with your drawer. Ah, but that's the whole point. The laws of arithmetic can tell you what you'll find with absolute certainty, *provided that* there's no interference (a thief, for example) . . . Aren't the laws of nature much in the same boat? Don't they tell you what will happen provided that there is no interference?[33]

If there is a God who made the world, it follows that he set up those laws in the first place. And if he is ever to break them would it not stand to reason that the occasion of his appearance on earth would be an obvious time to do so?

It is not as if reports of miracles like this were common in the first century. Those who witnessed them were astounded. After Jesus healed a man who was paralysed Mark tells us: "This amazed everyone and they praised God, saying, 'We have never seen anything like this!' "[34] Not long afterwards he spoke to a storm as one might address a naughty puppy: "Quiet! Be still!" and the wind died down instantly. The disciples were terrified and asked each other, "Who is this? Even the wind and the waves obey him!"[35] That is a great question to ask – who is this? Jesus was clear what he thought our answer should be: "Believe me when I say that I am in the Father and the Father is in me; or at least believe on the evidence of the miracles themselves."[36] The miracles point to the true identity of Jesus. He is who he said he was, the promised Messiah who had come to earth to establish God's kingdom.

Throughout the Bible we find God taking the initiative to make himself known. With the coming of Jesus that revelation reached its perfection. One Bible writer put it like this: "In the past God spoke to our forefathers through the prophets at many times and in various ways, but in these last days he has spoken to us by his Son."[37] This was the moment to which the whole Old Testament had been pointing – the time of fulfilment. Now at last the great promises of God could be fulfilled. The Christ had arrived – God's Son, the "wonderful counsellor, mighty God". That is quite a claim to make about a carpenter who died as a common criminal. But if it is right do you see what it means? We do not have to be in the dark about God any more, relying simply on our uncertain guesses. We can know the truth. Of course

Notes

1. Gene Edward Veith, *Guide to Contemporary Culture* (Crossway, 1994), 16.
2. *The Times*, 24-6-96.
3. The *Daily Telegraph*, December 1996.
4. Dave Tomlinson, *The post-evangelical* (Triangle, 1995), 78.
5. Quoted in Nick Pollard, *Why Do They Do That?* (Lion 1998), 25.
6. Quoted in Norman Anderson, *Christianity and Comparative Religion* (Tyndale Press, 1970), 14.
7. In Bertrand Russell, *Why I am not a Christian* (Routledge, 1992).
8. *The Sunday Times*, 17-1-93.
9. Mark 1:15.
10. Isaiah 9:6.
11. Isaiah 53:3.
12. Luke 4:21.
13. John 5:39.
14. Matthew 11:28.
15. John 14:6.
16. John 14:9.
17. John 10:30.
18. Mark 2:7.
19. C.S. Lewis, *God in the Dock* (Fount, 1998) 74.
20. *Ibid.*, 75.
21. *The Sunday Times*, 13-9-92.
22. Bruce (IVP, 1943); Barnett (Hodder, 1986).
23. 1 John 1:1.
24. 2 Peter 1:16.
25. Luke 1:1–4.
26. John Robinson, *Can We Trust the New Testament?* (Mowbrays, 1977).
27. Matthew 5:3; 5:43–44; 7:1.
28. *The Sunday Times*, 9-6-96.
29. Matthew 26:64.
30. Matthew 11:4–5.
31. Mark 3:22.
32. Bruce, *Are the New Testament Documents Reliable?*, 68.
33. From "Religion and Science", in *God in the Dock*.
34. Mark 2:12.

[35] Mark 4:39–41.
[36] John 14:11.
[37] Hebrews 1:1–2.

5

Dying to Meet You

Sting's song "Message in a Bottle" was a hit in the seventies and again when it was re-released in a cover version twenty years later. A man is alone on a desert island, convinced that he is the loneliest person in the world. In his longing to make contact with others he sends out a message in a bottle. No reply comes; only millions of similar messages from lonely, isolated individuals.

Perhaps there has never been a generation that feels so alone. A range of different social changes over the last few decades have combined to produce an alarming breakdown in community life. It is partly a result of technology. There is less and less need for social interaction these days. The computer and the telephone enable us to work, shop and even do our banking from home. Children do not need to meet with others to play – computer games provide hours of solitary amusement. One was even advertised recently with these words: "Not got any friends? Don't worry, with this game you don't need friends."[1] Those who do want to make contact with others can do so without ever actually having to meet them. Alistair Wightman of Edinburgh declared recently: "I'm in love, this is the real thing". He had never met the object of his desire, Doris Lui from Philadelphia. Their courtship had been conducted entirely on e-mail. Another couple got married in Los Angeles in 1996 in the first Internet wedding. They were five miles apart, blessed by a clergyman equidistant from them both, with a best man in New York, a maid of honour in Seattle and guests on several continents.[2] For those worried by the commitment required even by such "silicon friend-ships", the television soaps offer an even less demanding alternative. Many people are more involved in the lives of their favourite characters in Albert Square, Coronation Street or Brookside than they are with those who live next door. The result is a series of "virtual relationships", which may dull the sense of loneliness in the short term but cannot ultimately satisfy.

But the greatest cause of the sense of isolation that so many feel is surely the breakdown of family life. There was a sixfold increase in the divorce rate in Britain between 1960 and 1995.[3] Over a third of marriages end in that way, leaving 400 children a day to watch their families break up.[4] Lord Spencer has poignantly described the frequent train journeys he made with his sister Diana from one parent to the other after their divorce. One of the reasons that the Princess of Wales captured the nation's heart was that so many could identify with her. She may have had wealth and glam-our but beneath it all she remained that little girl lost – desperate for love.

Kurt Cobain, another of today's dead icons, had been a happy little boy. He used to march up and down the road outside his home banging his toy drum with a wide smile on his face. It was not long before he achieved fame and fortune with his band "Nirvana", but the smile had gone. He shot himself in April 1994 aged only twenty-five. A biographer made this comment about him: "His whole approach to performance was a scream for attention. It must have been galling to have achieved his ambition and realise it still wasn't enough. He could be ecstatic and experience the brief illusion of happiness. What Cobain never knew was contentment."[5] He never recovered from his parents' divorce. The smiling six-year-old drummer-boy became a young man riddled with insecurity. He made a fortune, achieved critical acclaim and became a global icon, but none of those things could satisfy his need for love.

That longing for love is very evident in our society today. It explains at least part of the whole modern obsession with image. Studies in America revealed that more than half of thirteen-year-old girls were unhappy with their bodies. By the age of seventeen the figure had risen to 78 per cent.[6] Men are not immune from such concerns, as is witnessed by the spiralling market for male "body products". Not long ago the cosmetics section in a department store was the woman's domain, but now there is just as much space given to the men. The men's grooming industry has grown by about 40 per cent since 1994 and is worth about £454 million. Men's magazines are also catching up with their female counterparts. In 1992 their total circulation was 200,000. By 1998 FHM alone was selling 644,000 copies, with *Loaded* not far behind with 441,000.[7] Such publications tell us what we should look like, which music we should listen to, what clothes we should wear. Not everyone chooses to follow the mainstream in these things – many prefer to adopt an "alternative" image, but the motivation is the same. It reflects a longing to be accepted – to belong, to be liked. That might bring a measure of security, but it is very fragile. Mike Starkey puts it well: "If self-identity is rooted in nothing deeper than a well-presented image and the affirmation received from others, it is easily destroyed . . . A faux-pas in your choice of trainers can mean a collapsed sense of personal worth."[8]

Others look to sex to provide the security and love that they need. The sexual revolution of the 1960s changed the morals of society in this area. More and more young people began having sex at a younger and younger age. In 1965, 33 per cent of eighteen-year-old boys and 17 per cent of girls had had sex. By 1977 the figures had risen to 69 per cent and 56 per cent and have continued to rise since.[9] The new permissive society promised "free love", but so often it has just increased insecurity and loneliness. Marilyn Monroe was in many ways the icon of the new age. She said once: "A sex symbol becomes a thing. I hate being a thing. I've never liked sex myself; I don't think I ever will. It seems just the opposite of love." Mike Starkey makes another shrewd comment in his book *God, Sex and Generation X*: "Most of my contemporaries no longer make love. They shag, bonk and screw – quickly, anonymously, lovelessly. The generation more pitifully searching for intimacy than any other in history has taken the central sacrament of interpersonal intimacy and killed it dead."[10]

We remain a generation looking for love. Bertrand Russell once wrote: "The root of the matter is a very old-fashioned and simple thing; a thing so simple that I am almost ashamed to mention it for fear of the derisive smile with which cynics will greet my words. The thing we lack, and the thing I need, is love." Freddie Mercury, the lead singer of Queen, said these words shortly before he died: "You can have everything in the world and still be the loneliest man and that is the most bitter type of loneliness. Success has brought me worldwide idolization and millions of pounds but it has prevented me from having the one thing we all need – a loving ongoing relationship." A student summed it all up when he said, "I feel that no-one has ever loved me. I don't even think I know what love is."

It is to such an age, insecure, lonely and looking for love, that God speaks a message of great joy through the next momentous event that we are considering. The Bible says: "This is what love is: it is not that we have loved God, but that he loved us and sent his Son to be the means by which our sins are forgiven."[11]

"Very rarely will anyone die for a righteous man, though for a good man someone might possibly dare to die. But God demonstrates his love for us in this: While we were still sinners, Christ died for us."[12] An old hymn puts it well:

> Here is love vast as the ocean,
> Loving kindness as the flood,
> When the Prince of life, our ransom,
> Shed for us his precious blood.[13]

Here is a quality of love that is unique. It may be that we are fortunate enough to have loving parents and many faithful friends, but sooner or later they will let us down. But God's love demonstrated on the cross is perfect, constant, eternally secure. That is good news for all people of all time. And it is not just comforting news – it is also urgent.

Let us start with the facts. One day in the early thirties AD, Jesus of Nazareth was sentenced to death by the Roman authorities and nailed to a cross. He hung there in agony for a few hours and then he died. Crucifixion was one of the most gruesome forms of execution ever devised by man. The Roman historian Cicero described it as "a most vile and disgusting punishment". "To bind a Roman citizen is a crime, to flog him is an abomination, to kill him is almost an act of murder. To crucify him is – what? There is no fitting word that can possibly describe such a deed . . . The very word 'cross' should be far removed not only from the person of a Roman citizen, but from his thoughts, his eyes and his ears."[14] How, then, could such an abomination become the great symbol of the Christian faith? How could the apostle Paul write: "May I never boast except in the cross of our Lord Jesus Christ"?[15] We are so used to seeing a cross around someone's neck or on a church building that we miss the shock of it. But what would you think if you saw a solid gold model of an electric chair as a lapel badge or a sculpture of a hangman's noose outside a building? Why is it that Christians are so obsessed with the shameful death of their founder? The focus on the death of Jesus was there from the beginning. There was no shame, no embarrassment about it; quite the opposite. Up to a third of the accounts of Jesus' life in the Gospels are taken up with his death. But it is not just Christ's followers who make much of his death. It is clear from the Gospels that Jesus himself taught that he had to die and saw it as part of his mission. Anyone who is serious about understanding what Christians believe needs to get to the bottom of this mystery. It was the great reformer Martin Luther who once said, "If you want to understand the Christian faith you must understand the wounds of Christ."

In December 1982, millions of television viewers were glued to their sets as they watched a man struggle for survival in the icy cold water of the Potomac River in Washington DC. The water was so cold that no one could possibly stay alive in it for more than a few minutes. A helicopter quickly reached the scene and let down a rope that could pull him to safety. The man grabbed hold of it but then, to the amazement of those watching, he quite deliberately let it go. The same thing happened five times until, exhausted, he went under. That just does not make sense. He had the chance to save his life, but he would not take it. Was he mad? We need to understand the whole picture before we say yes. A plane took off from the airport but the engines soon failed. It was forced to make an emergency landing on the river. The helicopter arrived to try to save the passengers who were all stranded in the freezing water. The man who took the rope was a strong swimmer. He took hold of it and then swam as quickly as he could to the nearest person to him. He gave him the rope and watched as he was pulled to safety. That happened five times until, exhausted, he could go on no more, and he died. What at first sight looks like a crazy waste of life suddenly makes a lot of sense when one understands the whole story.

Nearly 2000 years before that incident Jesus of Nazareth caused a sensation in Galilee and Jerusalem. Crowds flocked to him, drawn by his brilliant teaching and amazing miracles. The world was at his feet. If he was around today, every university in the world would long to have him as their professor of theology – he taught as no one else has ever taught. Every circus owner would long to have him as their star attraction – he could even turn water into wine. Every hospital would long to have him as their chief physician – he could heal the sick with a word. Jesus was on the verge of a brilliant future. But at the height of his powers he quite deliberately turned his back on the possibility of a successful career and headed for Jerusalem and what he knew would be certain death. He knew that the religious authorities hated him and were determined to kill him. His followers begged him not to go, but still he went. And this was no foolish miscalculation, no tragic accident. He said that it had to happen: "The Son of Man [his preferred title for himself] must suffer many things and be rejected by the elders, chief priests and teachers of the law, and he must be killed."[16] At first sight it does not make sense. The obvious question to ask is "Why?" "Why did he have to die?"

Why did Jesus have to die?

The Bible's answer is clear: He died for others. Like the death of the man in the Potomac River, Jesus' death only makes sense once one understands the whole picture. He died so that others might live.

As we saw in chapter two, it is our rebellion against God which is the root cause of all that is wrong in the world. Because God is a holy God who hates what is evil he cannot ignore our wrongdoing; in his justice he must punish it. The result is that ours is a world that is under his judgement. We can see the signs of that judgement all around us in the things that spoil life on earth. But, wonderfully, God continues to love us. In his love he has determined to put things right again and to call to himself a people who will enjoy life in a restored creation in perfect friendship with him once more.

That plan was first revealed to Abraham and it was partially fulfilled amongst his descendants, the people of Israel, as described in the Old Testament. But there was always something missing. It was true that they had the privilege of God's presence amongst them in the Temple, but they could only approach him once sacrifices had been offered and even then they could not get really close. Their relationship with God remained a distant one. Only the high priest could enter "the holy of holies" at the heart of the Temple, which was the focus of God's presence, and that was only once a year. The reason for this distance was the sin of the people. As long as they continued to do what was wrong they would never be able to enjoy a perfect relationship with him.

An unresolved question underlies all God's dealings with Israel in the Old Testament: How can a perfect, holy God have sinful people as his friends? He cannot simply ignore disobedience and sweep it under the carpet – that would be to imply that it *does* not matter, but it does matter. Because of his character, God must express his hatred of what is wrong. Once again, that is good news. It means that this universe is not governed by an amoral God who does not care about all the evil that we see around us. He does care very much, infinitely more than we do, and one day he will make sure that those who are responsible will be brought to account. Justice will be done. But the flipside of that is that we must face God's just anger for all the wicked things that we have said and thought and done – he cannot turn a blind eye to it. That is why his relationship with the Israelites in the Old Testament was always imperfect. In his love he wanted to bless them, but in his justice he had to keep his distance and express his displeasure at their disobedience. That judgement was seen most clearly when God evicted his people from their land and sent them to live in exile.

The continuing disobedience of humanity prevented the complete fulfilment of the promises of God. How could he enjoy a perfect friendship with human beings when his justice demanded that he punish them? Something had to be done about the problem of sin if the promises that God made to Abraham could be completely fulfilled.

Is it a problem that we can deal with ourselves? We like to think that it is. We assume that it is just a matter of pulling our socks up a bit. In our more humble moments we admit that we are not perfect, but we are not that bad either. Surely all we need to do is try a bit harder – a few more good deeds here, a few less bad words there? But the problem is more fundamental than that – superficial solutions will not do.

The story is told of a boy who managed to get a valuable porcelain vase stuck on his head when he was playing spacemen one day. His mother rang her husband at work to ask for advice. "Shall I break it?" "Don't you dare," came back the reply, "I had it valued at Sotheby's last week and it's priceless. Take him to casualty." She ushered the boy to the car, but it was not there. Then she remembered that it was being serviced and the awful truth dawned on her – she would have to take him by public transport. What would people think as she got on the bus with a boy who had a vase where his face should have been? She could not work out what to do. Then she had an idea – she would dress him in his school blazer and put the school cap on top.

Are we not rather like that with our human nature? There is something obviously wrong with us. We are fundamentally flawed, unable to obey God and live as we should and yet we try to pretend that all is well by perching the little cap of self-respect and dignity on our heads. Others are fooled into thinking that we are fine upstanding citizens; we may even fool ourselves, but God knows the truth. He sees us as we really are. He knows everything about us; even those long-hidden skeletons at the back of the cupboard of our lives. Whether we admit it to ourselves or not, we are guilty before God and must face his anger. We can never deserve his friendship and a place in heaven, the perfect world that he will make when he reverses the effects of the Fall. Even if we were able to live perfect lives between now and the day that we die, we would still deserve the punishment of God for the things we have done wrong in the past. And religion will not help us either. We may say our prayers and be regular in our attendance at church, mosque or temple, but that does not alter the fact that we disobey God and deserve his judgement. We have to face up to the humbling fact that we are helpless.

I remember seeing an item on the local news programme a few years ago about a cow that had got stuck down a well. It had been so busy chewing the cud that it failed to notice the large hole in front of it and down it went. It did not have spiderman hooves to help it clamber up the vertical walls. There was nothing it could do. It was entirely dependent on someone coming to its rescue. And that is what happened. The farmer appeared, went down the well to where the cow was, put a harness around it and pulled it to safety.

We are in a similar position – down a deep hole, cut off from God in our disobedience. Our only hope is if someone comes to rescue us; and that is what Jesus did. He did not come to earth simply as a moral teacher to tell us how to add the frills to our basically good lives. He came as a rescuer to deal with the problem of sin so that God his Father might at last be able to fulfil all his promises to his people without compromising his justice. The angel told Joseph that he should be given the name "Jesus", which means "the Lord saves" (or rescues) "because he will save his people from their sins".[17] Jesus himself expressed his mission in similar terms when he said: "The Son of Man came to seek and to save what was lost."[18] And it was on the cross that the rescue was achieved. That brings us to the next question: What happened on the cross? How did the death of Jesus deal with the problem of sin?

2: What happened on the cross?

At one level, that is an easy question to answer. Each of the Gospels describes the scene. Jesus was taken to a place in Jerusalem known as Golgotha. He was offered some wine to drink to help dull the pain but he refused it. Then they drove the nails through his hands and feet and strung him up on the cross. It was customary to put a notice above the dying criminal's head stating the nature of the crime for which he was being punished. Pilate had these words posted: "The King of the Jews". He did not look much like a king as he hung there in agony. The crowd jeered at him: "He saved others; let him save himself if he is the Christ of God, the Chosen One." As he grew weaker Jesus cried out, "My God, my God, why have you forsaken me?"[19] He died soon afterwards. Could this really have been the Son of God? The cross was conclusive proof to many first-century Jews that Jesus could not be the Messiah. How could God's King be allowed to suffer in this humiliating way?

But the Bible insists that there was more happening than could be seen by the human eye. The cross was not a tragic failure; it was a triumphant rescue. Do you remember God's dilemma, if I can put it in human terms? In his love he longed to forgive his people and enjoy friendship with them. But in his justice he could not ignore their wrongdoing and had to punish them. How could the demands of both his love and his justice be met? The answer is that they could only be met through the death of his Son – there was no other way.

Jesus came to earth to be born as a man and lived a perfect life. He was the one man who has ever lived who never did anything wrong, so he does not deserve to face separation from God his Father, which is the inevitable punishment for sin. And yet on the cross he willingly faced that punishment so that others need not. I deserved to be there, facing the righteous anger of God for my rejection and disobedience of him, but if I put my trust in Christ I can be sure that he hung there in my place. He died so that I might live.

For a number of months chickens had been stolen from an Indian camp and the chief was losing patience. He announced that when the culprit was found he should face fifty lashes. One night there was a commotion in the camp – the thief had been caught red-handed. He was taken to the chief's tent and the sentence was passed: "fifty lashes". It was a dark night and the thief had his clothes wrapped closely around him so that no one could see who he was. It was only as they were binding him to a stake to carry out the punishment that the flickering camp fire revealed his identity – he was the chief's son. Everyone looked to the father to see if he would have mercy. But he had given his word that the thief should be whipped and the sentence stood. The whipping was about to begin when, to everyone's amazement, the chief wrapped himself around his son so that he would take the full force of the lashes. Because he loved his son so much, he decided to take his punishment instead. No human illustration is perfect of course, but that takes us some way towards understanding what Jesus did when he died on the cross. He stood in the place of others.

We have already met examples of God providing a stand-in so that he could forgive his people. It happened at the Passover when he rescued the Israelites from Egypt. Their first-born sons were spared because a lamb had been killed instead. The sacrificial system operated in a similar way. The animal died as a substitute so that the one who offered it need not die but was free instead to continue a relationship with God. But an animal could never be an adequate substitute for a human being. The sacrifices in the Old Testament were not enough to make us right with God. The fact that they had to be repeated over and over again, day after day, proclaimed that fact. They pointed beyond themselves to the one perfect substitute that God was going to send, the one of whom Isaiah prophesied: "He was pierced for our transgressions, he was crushed for our iniquities . . . he was led like a lamb to the slaughter."[20] The Messiah could not simply be a mighty king; he had also to be a suffering servant if he was to deal with our greatest problem and save us from our sin. As Jesus hung on the cross he achieved what the Old Testament said he would do. There need be no more sacrifices. God's anger against the sin of his people has been dealt with once for all. The death of Jesus was completely sufficient to deal with every wrong thought, word or deed of all those who put their trust in him.

We are now in a position to understand the puzzle concerning those strange words of Jesus from the cross. It used to bother me that he had said, "My God, my God, why have you forsaken me?" Did he lose his faith at the crucial moment? Was this a declaration of despair? Not at all. He was stating a fact. He really was forsaken by his Father – that was the punishment that he took on behalf of others. But why did he say it in the form of a question? Simply because he is quoting a verse from the Old Testament which is found as a question. The words he used came straight from Psalm 22, a psalm of King David. The psalm speaks of a righteous man who suffers at the hands of others before ultimately being vindicated. There are a number of striking similarities between the psalm and the experience of Jesus on the cross. He quotes it for the same reason that he almost always quoted from the Old Testament – to show that he was the one to whom it pointed.

So, what happened on the cross? Jesus died to rescue God's people. God's love was satisfied – he was now able to call human beings back to himself and let them enjoy the full blessings of a perfect relationship with him, as promised to Abraham years before. But God's justice was also satisfied. He was now able to forgive without being open to the charge that he was going soft on evil. He has not ignored the sins of those he forgives – Jesus has already taken the punishment in their place. And remember who Jesus is – God himself in human form. God did not pick on some innocent third party and force him to die instead of others – that could never have been just. No, God directed his anger against himself in the person of his Son. He died so that we might live. The New Testament writers sum it up well:

> Christ loved me and gave himself up for me. He himself bore our sins in his body on the tree. For Christ died for sins once for all, the righteous for the unrighteous, to bring you to God.[21]

What are the results of Jesus' death?

The Bible presents the cross as the most important turning point of all – it is the hinge of history. There is space to consider just two of its consequences. As a result of Jesus' death, God's enemies are defeated and God's people are forgiven.

1: God's enemies are defeated

At the end of the nineteenth century the Ethiopians were finding it difficult to keep crime under control. Their ruler, Menelich the Second, heard of a special chair in

America that dealt very effectively with criminals and he promptly ordered two. The problem was that Ethiopia did not have electricity, so Menelich threw one of the chairs away and used the other as his throne. He ruled from an instrument of execution. The Bible teaches that the same is true of Jesus. He reigned from the cross – on it he achieved the greatest victory the world has ever seen.

Ever since humanity turned away from God at the Fall, life has been spoiled. God handed us over to the consequences of our disobedient choice. As a result, we are no longer free. We are bound by forces from which we cannot escape. Despite our progress in so many fields, we are still powerless in the face of sin, death and evil. Sin is presented in the Bible as a tyrant which has us in its grip.

There is a story from Australia which tells of a snake which managed to get into a house one day where it saw a canary in a cage. It licked its lips, or whatever a snake's equivalent is, and thought that the bird would make a very good lunch. It was not long before the bird had disappeared into its mouth. As it was happily digesting its meal the owners of the house returned. It was clearly time for a swift exit, but the snake had grown larger as a result of its lunch and it could no longer squeeze through the bars of the cage. It was trapped by its own greed.[22]

We are rather similar. Sin looks so attractive and we gobble it up. But then we find that it has trapped us. We cannot stop doing what is wrong, even when our conscience pricks us and we want to change. And the result is that we cannot escape from the inevitable consequence of our wrongdoing, the punishment of death, separation from God.

The Bible tells us that there is a supernatural power behind this captivity. The Bible never tells us how the devil came into being; it simply states that he exists. There is a supernatural world which includes a force for evil which is far stronger than we are. If we are to escape from the power of sin, death and evil we need God to defeat them for us so that the dominion of evil might be replaced by the kingdom of God. It was on the cross that he achieved that victory.

Jesus' miracles had already demonstrated that he had power over our enemies. We could see them as initial skirmishes in the war between God and the devil. But the decisive battle was fought and won when Jesus died. As a result of the cross, those who trust in Christ are set free from the old captivity. We are not trapped by sin any more because its penalty has already been faced for us. Just as at the Exodus the Israelites had been set free from slavery in Egypt, so Christians have been set free from the tyranny of sin. God's enemies are no longer able to get at us. The spiritual forces of evil have suffered an humiliating defeat and been rendered powerless. As the apostle Paul put it, "Having disarmed the powers and authorities, [God] made a public spectacle of them, triumphing over them by the cross."[23]

2: God's people are forgiven

The defeat of our enemies on the cross means that nothing now can stop God's plan to establish his kingdom. His promise to bring a people back to himself and to re-establish his rule on earth will be fulfilled. Anyone who trusts in Christ can belong to that people and will enjoy forever a place in the perfect world that God has promised to create in the future. We do not deserve such privileges one bit. For the sins of today we could rightly be banished forever from

God's presence. But the amazing truth is that it is possible for us to be forgiven, despite all that we have done wrong. A great exchange has taken place. Jesus identified himself with disobedient human beings and took the judgement we deserved so that, if we turn to him, we can receive the gift of a right relationship with God.

The humanist Marghanita Laski once said in a television discussion, "What I envy most about you Christians is your forgiveness. I have nobody to forgive me."[24] Kingsley Amis, the novelist, said much the same thing shortly before he died: "One of the great things about organised religion is that you can be forgiven your sins." Then he paused for a long time and bowed his head. "I mean, I carry my sins around with me. There's nobody to forgive them." But there is – Christ's death makes forgiveness possible for anyone, no matter how badly they have lived.

David Watson spoke at many universities throughout the 1970s. One evening as he was about to speak for a Christian Union he noticed a girl enter the room alone and stand at the back. There was something about her that drew his attention and he asked the chairman of the meeting who she was. He was amazed to see her there and said that she was one of the most notorious students in the college. She had the reputation of being someone who would do anything – drink anything, smoke anything, sleep with anyone. Throughout the talk she continued to smoke and look angry. At the end David invited anyone who wanted to accept Christ's forgiveness to pray a prayer with him. To his surprise the girl came forward and said she wanted to talk. They arranged to meet the next day. He hardly recognized her as she came through the door. The scowl of the previous evening had completely disappeared. David began by saying, "I gather you have a reputation for being the wildest student in the whole university." She replied, "It's true – there was nothing that I wouldn't do. But," she continued, "all along I felt as guilty as hell." Then a broad smile came over her and she said, "But now I've been forgiven and it's marvellous." She described how she had gone back to her room after hearing that Christ had died for her and just cried for hours – tears of joy. She could hardly believe that someone would love her that much. The death of Jesus meant life for her. Instead of being cut off from God and facing his anger she now knew that she had been welcomed by him into his family – totally accepted and forgiven. The same is true for all those who recognize their need before God and ask for his mercy because of what Christ has done.

For a number of years I lived just next to a pub, so close that I shared in whatever entertainment they provided, whether I liked it or not. Friday night was disco night. It followed a set pattern. The slow music would come on for the last half hour and always end with Whitney Houston's song "I will always love you". No doubt it made for a very romantic end to the evening as couples stared lovingly into each other's eyes. I sometimes wondered if any of them noticed the irony in the fact that many would be back the following week dancing to the same music but clutching a different partner. Love does not often last long these days. No wonder the student I mentioned earlier in the chapter could say, "I feel that no-one has ever loved me. I don't even think I know what love is." But we only need to look to the cross to find out. Christ died for those who had done nothing for him. The world has never seen a greater example of love than that. And when he says "I will always love you", we can be sure he means it.

Notes

1   Quoted in Pollard, *Why Do They Do That?*, 51.
2   *The Times*, 14-2-96.
3   Mike Starkey, *God, Sex and Generation X* (SPCK, 1997), 32.
4   Pollard, *Why Do They Do That?*, 48.
5   Christopher Sandford, *Kurt Cobain* (Vista, 1996).
6   *The Times*, 7-10-97.
7   *The Times*, 26-8-98 and *The Sunday Times*, February 1998.
8   Mike Starkey, *CPAS Magazine*, December 1997.
9   Mike Starkey, *God, Sex and Generation X*, 47.
10 Mike Starkey, *God, Sex and Generation X*, 45.
11 1 John 4:10 (*Good News Bible*).
12 Romans 5:7–8.
13 William Rees and William Edwards.
14 Quoted in John Stott, *The Cross of Christ* (IVP, 1986), 24.
15 Galatians 6:14.
16 Mark 8:31.
17 Matthew 1:21.
18 Luke 19:10.
19 Matthew 27:46; Mark 15:34.
20 Isaiah 53:5–7.
21 Galatians 2:20; 1 Peter 2:24; 1 Peter 3:18.
22 Roy Clements, *Introducing Jesus* (Kingsway, 1986), 92.
23 Colossians 2:15.
24 John Stott, *The Contemporary Christian* (IVP, 1992), 48.

6

The Day Death Died[1]

Three people die every second, 180 every minute, almost 11,000 every hour, about 260,000 every day and 95 million a year.[2] It has been described as the ultimate statistic: one in one dies. But despite its inevitability, very few of us ever talk about death. The Victorians had a morbid fascination with the subject but were very coy when it came to sexuality. We are the exact opposite. Sex is everywhere, but we keep death hidden as much as possible. Someone has put it well: "If the nineteenth century tried to conceal the facts of life, the twentieth tries to conceal the facts of death." We say, "She has kicked the bucket", "He has passed away", but hardly ever, "He's dead" – that sounds too blunt, too final. In the Middle Ages it was not unusual for prominent people to have a skull on their desks as a *"memento mori"*–a reminder of their mortality. We are very different today. The undertaker who is reported to have signed his letters, "Yours eventually," and said, "See you soon" when saying goodbye, will not have been popular. We prefer to hide death away in morgues and crematoria. Many of us have never seen a dead body. On the few occasions when we are forced to face death we tend to make light of it and pretend that it is not that bad after all. An advert for the Rosewood Memorial Park at Tidewater, West Virginia, said, "Now you can enjoy dying. Call today for information about clean, dry, ventilated entombment at special pre-construction prices!"[3]

This awkwardness concerning death reveals a deep-rooted fear. Peter Hall, the theatre director, said recently, "I do think about death every day and always have done."[4] Woody Allen famously said once: "It's not that I'm afraid to die; I just don't want to be around when it happens." The joke could not disguise the fear. In one interview he said: "The fundamental thing behind all motivation and all activity is the constant struggle against annihilation and death. It is absolutely stupefying in its terror, and it renders anyone's accomplishments meaningless." We are afraid not simply of the process of death and the uncertainty that lies beyond but also of its implications. Allen was surely right. If death is the end, then our few fleeting years on earth will be soon forgotten. It will not be long before no one will remember us at all. All that we strove for is rendered "meaningless". H.G. Wells saw that clearly: "If there is no afterlife, then life is just a sick joke, braying across the centuries."

Perhaps that explains the rise in the belief in reincarnation – anything is better than extinction. David Icke told the world in his book *Truth Vibrations* that he had first appeared on earth at the start of the Atlantis civilization. Since then, in the course of a long series of reincarnations, he was married in ancient Greece to a woman called Lucy, became the brother of the seventeenth-century philosopher Francis Bacon, was one of Napoleon's generals and a North American Indian chief. But what evidence is there for such wild claims?

Others prefer to put their faith in science. An increasing number of people are paying up to £60,000 to practitioners of "cryonics". The blood is drained from the corpse which is then filled with freezer fluid, encased in aluminium and suspended in a bath of liquid nitrogen. The hope is that a cure will be found for the disease that causes death which will enable life to be resumed after the body has been thawed.[5] It is a large investment for a very slim chance of a return.

This widespread fear of death is not surprising. The Bible teaches that it is an enemy – an alien intruder which was not part of God's original plan for the perfect world that he made. Human beings were not designed to die – death only entered the world after the Fall. You will remember that God told Adam and Eve that they could eat of any tree in the Garden of Eden except the tree of the knowledge of good and evil. The command came with a warning: "If you eat of it you will surely die."[6] It happened just as God had said. Once the first humans had eaten of the forbidden fruit God banished them from his presence and prevented them from returning to the tree of life. The symbolism is powerful. Death is the result of human rebellion against God. From now on human beings would be mortal. As the apostle Paul put it in the New Testament: "The wages of sin is death".[7]

We have seen in the last two chapters that the Bible proclaims Jesus to be the great rescuer who has come from God. He came to undo the effects of the Fall and to introduce the kingdom of God, in which everything is restored to its perfection and the world is once again as it was designed to be. To make that possible he had to deal with the fundamental problem – our sin and God's righteous anger against it. That he achieved by his death on the cross. But how can we be sure that the death of one man all those years ago really was the key turning point of history? Why should we believe that he achieved a great victory there which changes everything? The Bible's answer is to point us to the resurrection of Jesus from the dead. Death is the great sign of the judgement of God. Death spoils this world, but it has been defeated. We need not fear it any more; instead we can have hope as we face the future. And that hope is not based on mere wishful thinking; it is firmly rooted in an historical event: the first Easter Day – the day death died.

The Christian claim

Varsity and *Cherwell*, the university newspapers of Oxford and Cambridge, conduct annual surveys. One year the results reached the front page of *The Independent*: "Students say the person they most admire is Christ and their favourite book is the Bible. Going to church rates among their favourite activities along with drinking, socialising and listening to music." Jim Murphy, President of the National Union of Students, commented that the newly revealed popularity of Jesus and the Bible was "bizarre". "I am surprised and shocked. I have never heard anything like it before."[8] The survey the following year showed the same result. Jesus topped the poll for favourite hero or heroine, beating such luminaries as Margaret Thatcher, Kurt Cobain, Richard Dawkins and Dylan from *The Magic Roundabout*. Jesus lived and died nearly 2000 years ago and yet still he has a huge impact on our world – Jesus lives on.

A *Sunday Times* article about Freddie Mercury ended with these words: "So, Freddie is not dead. He may not have been spotted in as many supermarkets as Elvis, but his fans are just as reluctant to let him go. Pop stars are immortal because they provide the soundtrack for other peoples' lives."[9] Many famous figures from history live on in that sense – their influence continues. But the Christian claim is that Jesus does not just live on in the minds of his followers. He really is alive. He died but then he was raised from the dead, never to die again. That is why, down the ages, Christians have been able to say they know him as a living presence in their lives.

It had been an excellent first week of our family holiday in the Dordogne in southern France. My parents, twin sister and I had all got on well – there was remarkably little tension. But then my elder sister arrived. We picked her up from the train station and it was as we were returning to the camp site that she said it: "You aren't real Christians you know." She had been an earnest Christian since starting at university and we had talked before about her faith but she had never been as blunt as this. I was livid and started shouting at her. How dare she suggest that we were not Christians? After all, we lived pretty decent lives compared to many people and we even went to church fairly regularly. What arrogance to imply that she was a Christian and we were not! The rest of the journey passed in an awkward silence. I hardly spoke to her for the rest of the week – the holiday had been spoilt. The Sunday after we returned home she decided that she wanted to go to a church in the local town which had been recommended to her and she asked me to drive her. It was the last thing I wanted to do but my mother pointed out that I had been so beastly to her over the previous few days that it was the least I could do and it might shut her up.

I felt uncomfortable throughout the whole service but I was struck by what I saw and heard. The minister began by announcing some sad news. A child, whose parents were church members, had been killed in a bicycle accident the previous day. Another couple stood up to pray for this family. Before they began they said that something very similar had happened to them a few years before. They had lost a much-loved child and were devastated, but they spoke movingly about how Jesus had been very close to them in their grief and had helped them through. It was then that I realized that my sister had been absolutely right, even if she had not been tactful. Here were people who talked of a personal relationship with Jesus and of him making a difference in their lives, even in painful circumstances. They claimed to know him. I knew nothing of that. My Christianity was limited to going to church from time to time and trying to live a decent life. It was then that I resolved to look into the Christian faith for myself and make my own decision about it, one way or the other. I began by reading one of the New Testament Gospels. As I did so I found myself being drawn very strongly to the person of Jesus. He spoke to me not as a voice from the dead but as a living presence. I became convinced that he was alive and that he was calling me to follow him. I have been doing so for fifteen years now and I am as convinced now as I was then that Jesus is alive – he has changed my life. Countless Christians could say the same.

The evidence for the resurrection

It is all very well to talk of Christian experience but could we not be deluded? People believe all sorts of strange things with great conviction but that does not make them true. Is there any historical evidence for the resurrection? Yes there is. I will focus on just two facts.

1: The tomb was empty

Jesus died on a Friday. The next day was the Jewish Sabbath which was strictly observed by the Jews as a day of rest, so it was on the Sunday that some women went to the tomb to attend to Jesus' body and put spices on it. When they arrived they found that the body had disappeared. At least five disciples are recorded as having witnessed the strange scene. The linen cloths which had been wrapped round the body were still there, undisturbed, but there was nothing inside them. What happened to that body? A number of suggestions have been made.

Grave robbers stole it

• But why would they have picked on the only tomb in Jerusalem that was guarded? And why take the one thing that was worthless, the body, and leave the cloths and the spices, the only items of any value in that tomb? There was no anatomy department in Jerusalem desperate for bodies to dissect. That body would have been useless to them.

The women went to the wrong tomb

• But Mark's Gospel tells us quite specifically that they had seen where he had been buried.[10] And is it not highly unlikely that the reports of Jesus' resurrection would have been allowed to persist without someone going to the correct tomb and pointing out that the body was still there?

The Roman authorities stole the body

• No doubt they knew that Jesus had said that he would rise again after his death, so perhaps they took the body into safe keeping to prevent any of his disciples stealing it and then claiming that he had risen? That would have prevented any chance of another troublesome religious cult emerging. But if they had done that why did they not produce the body when news of the resurrection began to spread? That would have killed the rumours stone dead.

The disciples stole it

- They had staked their lives on their belief that Jesus was the Messiah. No doubt their parents had said that it was just a phase they were going through and their friends had laughed at their religious fervour. And when Jesus died they realized that they had indeed been fools. They could not face owning up and going back home and saying, "Mum, Dad, you were right all along – he was a fraud", so they decided to pretend that he had risen from the dead. They stole the body, hid it and then started proclaiming that he was the risen Messiah. But does that really make sense? Even the most basic knowledge of human psychology would tell you that they really believed that he was alive. Why else would they have gone to such great efforts to spread the news about him, to the extent that they were often martyred for their faith? People may die for what is not true, but would they really have died for what they knew was not true – because they had invented it?

2: *Jesus appeared to his followers*

Over a period of six weeks Jesus appeared to different groups of his followers on at least ten occasions. At one time he was seen by 500 people at once. Paul tells us that most of them were still alive as he wrote – in other words, those who did not believe him could go and ask them.[11] They were not naïve gullible individuals who found it easy to believe that a dead man had come back to life; it was just that there was no other explanation. Thomas, the sceptic, had not been present when Jesus appeared to the other disciples. He would not believe what they told him: "Unless I see the nail marks in his hands and put my finger where the nails were, and put my hand into his side, I will not believe it." A week later Jesus came again. He said to Thomas, "Put your finger here; see my hands. Reach out your hand and put it into my side. Stop doubting and believe." Thomas simply replied, "My Lord and my God."[12]

These extraordinary events were not invented – I have argued already that it is clear that the first Christians were convinced that Jesus had risen. What possible explanations are there?

Jesus had not died

- He looked dead, so the soldiers took him down from the cross and put him in the tomb. But once there, the cool air revived him; he pushed the stone away from the entrance and escaped. It was this revived Jesus, rather than the risen Jesus, that the disciples saw. But is that really plausible? Is it possible that a man who had been flogged, hung on a cross for six hours, lost consciousness and been in a tomb for three days without food or medical help, could have revived? And even if he had done so, it is hardly likely that he could have persuaded anyone that he had conquered death – he would have been barely alive.

The disciples hallucinated

- But hallucinations almost always come to those who are longing for something to happen – as a wish-fulfillment. The disciples, by their own admission, had not been expecting the resurrection. And hallucinations are very individual – not shared in every detail by groups, as in the New Testament accounts. Furthermore, the risen Jesus could be seen, heard and touched. He had detailed conversations with people. He even ate some fish!

Jesus had indeed risen from the dead

- As I examined the evidence for the resurrection for the first time, I came to see that it was far easier to believe that Jesus had risen than to believe the alternatives – it is amazing what you have to believe to not believe. All the evidence supports the claims of those first disciples. How else can one explain the astonishing change in them? After Jesus was arrested they were dejected and close to despair. They had hoped that he was the Messiah, but now all their dreams had been dashed as they had seen him die a humiliating death. They were petrified that the next knock on the door would be the Roman authorities arresting them for following Jesus. But something happened to change this pathetic rabble into men of such power that they turned the world upside down by their preaching. And then there was Saul, a vicious opponent of the newly flourishing Christian movement. What changed him into the great apostle Paul who became the greatest of the early Christian preachers? It was the fact of the resurrection. "Last of all," he wrote, "he appeared to me."[13]

The consequences of the resurrection

The resurrection is another of the great turning points of history. It has enormous repercussions for us and for our world. We will consider two.

1: Jesus really is the promised Messiah

18 June 1815 is one of the most significant dates in British history – the day on which Wellington faced Napoleon at Waterloo. The future of the nation was at stake. People up and down the country were on tenterhooks – everyone was waiting to hear what had happened. One of the main lookout posts was the roof of Winchester Cathedral, from where the channel could just be seen. At last the signal ships came into view. A severe fog almost prevented the signal from being visible. But before the mist finally came down, the essentials of the message could just be made out: "WELLINGTON DEFEATED." The worst had happened, and the depressing news began to spread from beacon to beacon. A few hours later, the fog lifted, and only then could the full message be seen: "WELLINGTON DEFEATED THE FRENCH."

It would be hard to find a more pathetic picture of weakness than Jesus on the cross. He did not look like the great Messiah that he had declared himself to be. His miracles had suggested that he might indeed have been the mighty king promised by the prophets, but his death seemed to put an end to that idea. The paintings sanitize the scene, but make no mistake – it was not pretty. It was full of blood and tears and sweat. Every breath Jesus took sent the pain stabbing through his body as he had to lift himself up on the nails. And all the time he was surrounded by a jeering mob who were enjoying the spectacle. No doubt they laughed at the crown of thorns on his head and the mocking sign above him: "The King of the Jews". Some king! As far as they were concerned, the message of the cross was crystal clear: "JESUS DEFEATED". But how wrong they were. That twisted, agonized figure was and is the Lord of life, and in his death he was achieving the greatest victory the world has ever seen. That victory was only proclaimed two days later when, on the first Easter Sunday, he rose from the dead. Then, at last, could the full message be seen: "JESUS DEFEATED THE GRAVE". Jesus was not just a religious teacher; he was and is the mighty, victorious Messiah. The resurrection reveals the true identity of Jesus. As Paul wrote to some Christians in Rome, "He was declared with power to be the Son of God, by his resurrection from the dead."[14] His friends buried him in a tomb, but God raised him to a throne. It was the great vindication of all that he had said about himself. Once we recognize the truth of the resurrection we should all use the words of Thomas: "My Lord and my God."

2: Jesus really is introducing the new age

The hope held out by the prophets was nothing less than the transformation of everything. When the Messiah came he would bring an end to this present world, spoilt by our rebellion against God, and introduce a new age, the kingdom of God, in which everything is restored to its perfection – life as it was meant to be. On the cross Jesus achieved the victory against God's enemies that made that possible. But that victory was not evident until the resurrection. The fact that Jesus rose from the dead proved that death had indeed been conquered – Jesus defeated the grave. "Death has been swallowed up in victory. Where, O death, is your victory? Where,

O death, is your sting?"[15] The fact that Jesus defeated death does not simply show that he is the Messiah; it also proves that he is able to introduce the new age that the prophets had promised. The resurrection marked the beginning of that new age. It proved that there was life beyond death.

For many years Europeans believed that there was no land to the west of Portugal. There was a large plaque in the port of Lisbon which simply said: "Ne plus ultra" – "Nothing beyond this". But, as you know from your history at school, "In fourteen hundred and ninety-two, Columbus sailed the ocean blue" and discovered America. When he returned to Portugal the plaque was changed. It now read: "Plus ultra" – "There *is* more beyond this".

Before the resurrection there was no hope of anything beyond death. This world was trapped "in bondage to decay".[16] Sin led inevitably to death and eternal separation from God, and there was nothing that could be done about it. But Jesus changed all that. On the cross he took the penalty for sin upon himself and, as a result, the power of death was broken. It was now possible for God to introduce the new age, marked not by death but by life – eternal life in relationship with him. It is the resurrection that proclaims that possibility: "Plus ultra" – "There is more beyond this".

The new age has not been fully introduced yet, but the process which will lead in time to the new creation has begun with the resurrection. C.S. Lewis expressed this truth powerfully in one of his essays:

> To be sure, it feels wintry enough still: but often in the very early spring it feels like that. 2000 years are only a day or two by this scale. A man really ought to say 'the resurrection happened' in the same spirit in which he says 'I saw a crocus yesterday'. The spring comes

slowly down this way; but the great thing is that the corner has been turned.[17]

Elsewhere he writes: "He has forced open a door that has been locked since the death of the first man. He has met, fought and beaten the King of Death. Everything is different because he has done so. This is the beginning of the new creation. A new chapter in cosmic history has opened."[18]

The New Testament teaches that, because Jesus has defeated death, all those who trust in him can share in his victory. They can die with the confidence that death is not the end. There is life beyond the grave. That explains the remarkable assurance and peace that so many Christians have shown in their final days on earth. John Rogers was burnt for his faith in 1555. The French ambassador witnessed the scene. He said later that Rogers had walked to his death "as if he was walking to his wedding." I think of Mark Ruston, a vicar in Cambridge for many years, who had a deep impact on the lives of many undergraduates, including mine. He had retired and knew that he was dying of cancer. It would have been easy to dwell on the past, but he had his eyes fixed firmly on the future and he was able to say: "The best is yet to come". The twinkle in his eyes as he said those words confirmed to me that he really believed them. He wrote to a friend a month before he died: "I cannot honestly say that I look forward to the last bit of the journey, but beyond that I know that I shall see Christ, and what could compare with that?"

Bertrand Russell once said that Christian optimism about the future life is "built on the ground that fairy tales are pleasant".[19] Is that all that the hope of John Rogers, Mark Ruston, and countless other Christians consists of? Were they simply clutching at straws?

No – their confidence was built on solid ground. Peter, one of the first disciples, wrote: "Praise be to the God and Father of our Lord Jesus Christ, who in his great mercy has given us new birth into a living hope, through the resurrection of Jesus Christ from the dead."[20] It is the fact of the resurrection that is the foundation of Christian hope. The decisive battle has been won; it is now only a matter of time before the full fruits of that victory are enjoyed forever.

A History of the World

The story so far:

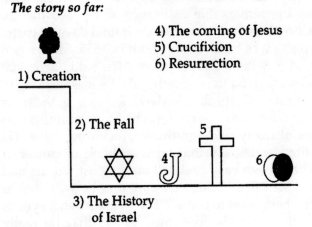

1) Creation

2) The Fall

3) The History of Israel

4) The coming of Jesus
5) Crucifixion
6) Resurrection

Notes

1 The title of a book on the resurrection by Michael Green (IVP, 1982).
2 John Blanchard, *Whatever Happened to Hell?* (Evangelical Press, 1993), 46.
3 David Watson, *Is Anyone There?* (IVP, 1979), 65.
4 *The Sunday Times*, 1-3-92.
5 Blanchard, *Whatever Happened to Hell?*, 47.
6 Genesis 2:17.
7 Romans 6:23.
8 *The Independent*, 11-12-95.
9 *The Sunday Times*, 17-11-96.
10 Mark 15:47.
11 1 Corinthians 15:6.
12 John 20:25–28.
13 1 Corinthians 15:8.
14 Romans 1:4.
15 1 Corinthians 15:54–55.
16 Romans 8:21.
17 From "The Grand Miracle" in *God in the Dock* (Fount, 1998), 58.
18 From *Miracles* (Fontana, 1947), 149.
19 Quoted in Michael Green, *The Empty Cross of Jesus* (Hodder, 1984), 132.
20 1 Peter 1:3.

7

Starting All Over Again

Golf must be the most infuriating game ever devised – it is designed to keep us humble. I always start a round full of confidence. I have my trusty clubs in the bag, new balls, a smart trolley; the sun is shining, life is good. Surely this will be the day when I break my record and have the round of a lifetime; nothing can go wrong. But it is not long before the smile is replaced by my usual golfing scowl as I return to the familiar "military golf" – left, right, left, right. Left into the bushes, then right into the trees; not exactly the direct route to the green. It is at that moment that I long to go back to the beginning and start again. It would be lovely to be able to nip back down the first fairway and tee off as if nothing had happened. But it cannot be done – golfing etiquette will not allow it. It is too late.

If you do not know that experience from golf, you will almost certainly have experienced something similar in an exam. There is that awful moment when the invigilator has just announced that there are five minutes left and only then do you suddenly realize that you have completely missed the point of the first two essay questions. You have a great urge to scrumple up the bits of paper and start again but it is too late – there is no time left.

Sometimes we all feel like that with life. We have made mistakes. Perhaps particular things come to mind as we look back: a spoilt relationship, ruined by our selfish behaviour; a wasted opportunity, gone now; some unkind words that we have long regretted but we cannot take them back and the damage has been done. It would be marvellous to be able to blot them out and start all over again – what a wonderful thought that is! Tennyson spoke for many when he wrote, "O that a man might arise in me, that the man I am might cease to be." And it is not just we as individuals who need a fresh start like that. Our whole world has been ruined and is a long way from the perfection with which it was created. Is there any chance of a new beginning? Yes there is! It was made possible by the death and resurrection of Christ, as we have seen in the last two chapters. The next great turning point in God's history advances that process: the day of Pentecost.

What events would you include if you were asked to write a short history of the world? So much has happened in the history of the human race. What incidents would you single out as being especially significant? It is very likely that you would focus on moments that introduced a sea change, a whole new era. Perhaps the fall of Rome in 410, the fall of Constantinople in 1453, the first printing press in 1476, or the invention of computers in the last few decades. I wonder if you would find a place for the day of Pentecost? I doubt it. I have two histories of the world on my shelves: Hendrik van Loon's *The Story of Mankind*[1] and H.G. Wells' *A Short History of the World*.[2] Both mention Jesus of Nazareth in passing, but there is nothing about this particular day. And yet the Bible makes it clear that it was a day of monumental significance; it was another of the great turning points in history.

Pentecost was an annual festival when the harvest was celebrated. Many Jews from all over Israel and beyond would converge on Jerusalem for the big event. Luke describes what the Christians saw on this particular Pentecost in the book of Acts in the New Testament. All the disciples were together when there was a sudden great noise. This was followed by a blaze of light and flame everywhere and "they saw what seemed to be tongues of fire that separated and came to rest on each of them."[3] They then began to speak in foreign languages that they had never spoken before. It is no wonder that these extraordinary events began to draw a crowd. Jews from all over the known world were there and they were amazed that these simple Galileans were able to praise God in their own languages. They did not have a degree in languages or even an A level between them, yet here they were speaking fluently with words that they had never used before and had not learnt – it was all very peculiar. It is hardly surprising that Luke records those who witnessed these things as being "amazed and perplexed".[4] Some even thought that the disciples were drunk, although I am not sure how that would explain their sudden ability to speak foreign languages. They were confused and needed an explanation of what was going on. It was Peter who stood up to provide it. He explained that they were witnessing the beginning of a new era: God had sent his Holy Spirit to his people just as he had said he would through the prophets years before.

Who is the Holy Spirit?

In one of the weddings in *Four Weddings and a Funeral*, Rowan Atkinson plays a nervous, blundering young vicar who is taking the service. With great reverence he prays in the name of "the Father, the Son and the Holy Goat" – that conjures up a wonderful image! The original is almost as peculiar. As a child I used to imagine "the Holy Ghost" as some spooky presence in a sheet floating around the place doing weird and wonderful things – a strange, elusive, impersonal force. But the Holy Spirit is not impersonal. The Bible refers to the Spirit as "he" or "him", not "it".[5] It describes him as doing things that only a person can do: he speaks, thinks and can be grieved.[6] He is personal because he is God.

Shortly before Jesus was arrested and crucified he reassured his disciples. Even though he was about to leave them, they would not be left on their own: "I will ask the Father and he will give you another Counsellor to be with you for ever."[7] That word "counsellor" translates a word in the original Greek which means "one who is called alongside". It was used to refer to a friend who was always there for you – "a right-hand man". While Jesus was on earth he had been that supporter and encourager for his disciples. Now that he is leaving, the Holy Spirit is to take his place. But, a sentence or two later, Jesus goes on to say, "I will not leave you as orphans; I will come to you."[8] It is by his Spirit that Jesus enters the lives of his disciples and strengthens them. The Spirit has even been described as "Jesus' other self". Elsewhere he is called "the Spirit of Christ" and "the Spirit of God".[9]

We saw in chapter 3 how God came close to the people of Israel and lived among them in the Temple in Jerusalem. That was an amazing privilege – God did not live with any other nation in that way. But still they could not enjoy an intimate relationship with him. The Temple declared both the nearness of God and his distance. It was full of a whole series of "No Entry" signs.

The first said "No Gentiles" – only Jews were allowed in the outer court. Then, "No women" – only Jewish men could enter the next courtyard. Next, "No laymen" – only the priests could go into the inner court. Finally, at the heart of the Temple, was the "Holy of Holies", the focal point of God's symbolic presence. Only one man, the High Priest, was allowed to enter there, and then only once a year. It is said that they used to tie rope around his feet in case he died in the presence of God – that would enable them to pull him out without going in themselves. It must have been tantalizing – God was so close to them and yet so far. The problem was their sin; there was no way that a sinful people could have an intimate relationship with the holy God.

They did get a hint every now and then of what they were missing when God, by his Spirit, came down to live not just in a building but in a person. But that did not happen very often and only a few people were affected – the odd king here, the odd prophet there. And the Spirit did not stay for long – he came and went. It was all very frustrating. But the prophets in the Old Testament made it clear that it would not be like that for ever. They spoke of a new age, a new era at the end of time, when God would intervene decisively in his world. He would come to judge his enemies and to save his people, people not just from Israel but from all nations. And they spoke of how God would deal with their sin. He would forgive them and bring them into a perfect relationship with him by his Spirit. There was Ezekiel, for example, writing at the time of the exile in Babylon and reporting this message from God:

> I will give you a new heart and put a new spirit in you;
> I will remove from you your heart of stone and give you
> a heart of flesh. And I will put my Spirit in you and move

you to follow my decrees and be careful to keep my laws.[10]

Joel also prophesied the sending of the Spirit:

And afterwards,
  I will pour out my Spirit on all people.
Your sons and daughters will prophesy,
  your old men will dream dreams,
  your young men will see visions.
Even on my servants, both men and women,
  I will pour out my Spirit in those days.[11]

That was a great promise! In the past only a few had the privilege of receiving God's Spirit – a small number of kings and prophets. But in the future all God's people would be able to have an intimate relationship with him by his Spirit – young and old, male and female. That was made possible by the death of Jesus which dealt with sin, the great barrier that cuts us off from God. It was no coincidence that as Jesus was dying the curtain in the Temple, which separated the Holy of Holies from the rest of the building, was "torn in two from top to bottom".[12] God was providing a magnificent visual aid – the "No Entry" signs had been taken down. The stage was set for the fulfilment of the prophets' promise – the sending of the Spirit to be with all God's people. It was on the day of Pentecost, a few weeks after Jesus' death and resurrection, that it finally happened.

Peter explained the strange events of that day by referring back to the Old Testament. "This is what was spoken by the prophet Joel: 'In the last days, God says, I will pour out my Spirit on all people.' "[13] That is why all those Christians were suddenly able to speak in other languages. It is not something we can expect to happen again – it was a one-off, marking a unique event. A whole new era in God's dealings with humanity had begun – a fresh start. From now on God's people need not go to the Temple to meet with him. No, God will come to live with them by his Spirit. He is not found in special buildings – it is God's people who are the dwelling place of God on earth. Paul reminds the Christians in Corinth of that wonderful truth in these striking words: "Do you not know that your body is a temple of the Holy Spirit, who is in you, whom you have received from God?"[14]

The Holy Spirit had been sent by God the Father and he has been with all God's people ever since.

What does the Holy Spirit do?

1: *He brings new life*

The Bible uses some strong images to describe our spiritual state without Christ. We are blind, enslaved and dead.[15] There is no point going to a blind man and telling him about a wonderful sunset and urging him, "Look at it; look at it!" – he can't! It is not tactful to speak to a prisoner behind bars and say, "Come on, out you come, this way" – he can't! And I do not advise going up to a corpse in a morgue and shouting, "Get a life!" – it can't! That, says the Bible, is how helpless we are. If we want to get right with God it will not be enough for us to pull up our socks and try a bit harder. As those who are blind, enslaved and dead, we are helpless – we need a miracle. Jesus has done everything to make that possible. He died on the cross in the place of others so that, if they trust in him, they can be sure that he took the punishment that they deserved.

So, all I have to do is receive by faith the gift of for-giveness that Christ offers me. But there's the rub – how can I? I am a disobedient rebel, rotten to the core. It is not in my nature to turn to him but rather to disobey him. I am spiritually dead. It will take a miracle for me to turn from my rebellion against God and instead to put my trust in Christ. The Holy Spirit has been sent by God to make that miracle possible. He has the power to bring new life to those who are spiritually dead.

Nicodemus was one of the Jewish religious leaders. No doubt he was often in the synagogue and observed the disciplined religious practices of a committed Jew. And yet Jesus said to him, "You must be born again."[16] That is not flattering. Imagine that news of my soccer talents finally reach the England football manager. He invites me to the Bisham Abbey training centre to show off my skills. After a while I ask him what he thinks – "Am I in, boss?" He shakes his head, so I ask him, "Is there anything I need to work on that would make a difference? Heading? My left foot?" Again he shakes his head and says, "Frankly, Vaughan, you need to be born again." I would not leave full of hope. He is telling me in the clearest language that there is nothing I can do. There is no point me putting in some extra training – I need to be a completely different per-son if I am to get into that team – and that is impossi-ble. Jesus says the same to Nicodemus. If he is to enter the kingdom of God and be right with him, he must be born again – he needs a new life. If that is true of a man like Nicodemus, who was well-known for his piety, it is certainly true of the rest of us. We need a miracle if we are to be accepted by God. The good news is that the Holy Spirit has been sent by God to make that miracle possible. As Jesus spoke with Nicodemus he made it clear that the Spirit could bring new birth.[17] It is possible to have a fresh start and to begin all over again.

The landlord looked very suspicious when I first suggested the idea. "Why do you want church in a pub?" he said, "You've got a perfectly good building of your own." I explained that there were many people who were interested in talking about the Christian faith but who would feel uncomfortable coming to a church service. He looked doubtful, but agreed to let us give it a go. We have been at it ever since. The aim is to provide as natural a setting as possible in which to discuss Jesus and his relevance today. Drinks are available at the bar and a meal is served. As people are eating there is a short talk which provides the subject for the evening's discussion, which takes place around the tables over coffee. Hundreds have come to the "Tavern" and many of them have received the new life that Jesus offers.

Joanna was consumed with bitterness towards some of her husband's family for things they had said and done in the past. As she came to the meetings she began to understand how she had hurt God by her behaviour towards him over many years, and yet he had still loved her – he sent his Son to die for her. She was amazed by such undeserved love and she accepted the forgiveness God offered her. She knew immediately that she could not go on resenting her relatives any more. Gradually she learnt to forgive. You could see it in her face – she had a new light in her eyes.

Peter was the life and soul of every party in his college. He was well-known for his drinking exploits and womanizing – the last person that his friends would have expected to go to a Christian meeting. But he came, and kept coming. Over a few weeks he became convinced that Jesus was who he claimed to be and that he had to follow him. His life changed dramatically.

Jason was asked to the "Tavern" by one of his friends in the sports club. He believed there probably was a God, but he was not at all religious. He had noticed that a number of the Christians he knew were different from everyone else. They had more time for others and they seemed to have their lives under control, so he went along to try to find out why. We look at Mark's Gospel during our meetings and Jason decided to read it for himself. In the past he had assumed that the Bible was a very dull, outdated book but now he found that he could not put it down. He was very struck by the person of Jesus and felt strongly drawn to him. It was as he read that he decided to follow Christ.

Laura had been going to church for as long as she could remember – it was one of those things that she just did. But it made no difference to her life in the rest of the week. She came to the "Tavern" because she thought it was time she thought things through for herself and came to her own conclusions about what she believed. It was the cross that struck her above all. No one had ever explained to her before why Jesus had died. She began to believe that he had died for her, taking the punishment that she deserved. That great truth changed her life. If Christ had done so much for her, how could she ignore him for most of the week? She became a whole-hearted follower of Jesus, even going on a mission team to Eastern Europe after finishing university.

There are just four individuals whose lives have been turned upside down by the Christian message. Countless others could tell a similar story of a new start in life. We are all different; for some it takes place over months, for others it happens dramatically in one evening, but in every case it is the Holy Spirit who has made it possible. On our own we would never recognize our need of Christ, but the Spirit was sent to "convict the world of guilt."[18] He helps us to acknowledge the serious position we are in as rebels against God who deserve nothing but his anger. But he does not leave us in despair – he points us to Jesus as the one who can rescue us. The Spirit does not draw attention to himself. He has been likened to a floodlight. It would be very strange to go to listen to a band at an evening concert and spend all the time staring at the lights. Their purpose is to illumine what is happening on the stage. In a similar way, the Spirit does not want us to focus on him; he points away from himself, just as Jesus said he would: "When the Counsellor comes, whom I will send to you from the Father, the Spirit of truth who goes out from the Father, he will testify about me."[19] He could almost be described as a matchmaker – he introduces us to Jesus. Are you beginning to see that you have done wrong and that God is rightly angry with you? And are you sensing that Jesus has been sent by God the Father to bring you forgiveness? If so, that is the work of the Holy Spirit – we could never believe such things without his help. Every time a person truly turns to Christ and begins to follow him, a miracle has taken place, achieved by God the Spirit.

It is humbling to recognize that – we do not find it easy to acknowledge that we are helpless on our own. But it is also encouraging. As those who are spiritually blind, enslaved and dead, we will never turn to Christ on our own. But God has not left us on our own – he has sent his Holy Spirit. What is impossible for us is possible for him; there is hope for us all. If you are serious about discovering whether or not the Christian faith is true, you should ask for God's help to understand. And you can be confident that the Holy Spirit will help you. Jesus himself gave this wonderful promise: "Ask and it will be given to you; seek and you will find; knock and the door will be opened to you. For everyone who asks receives; he who seeks finds; and to him who knocks, the door will be opened."[20] You too could receive a fresh start in life and be "born again". The apostle Paul knew the truth of that. He had been changed from a hateful persecutor of Christians into a loving disciple of Christ. No wonder he could say: "If anyone is in Christ, he is a new creation; the old has gone, the new has come!"[21]

The Holy Spirit brings new life by drawing people to Christ in the first place. But his work does not end there. Having introduced an individual to Christ, he continues to work in their life giving them the power they need to live the Christian life.

2: He gives power to change

"But I could never keep going", said John as he sat in my study. He had been thinking about the Christian faith for a while and had become convinced that it was true. But still he did not commit his life to Christ. He knew that there would have to be changes. He was not a particularly bad person, but there were many things in his life which did not fit with the teaching of Jesus. What was the point in even trying to change them? He had made attempts at self-reformation before – every New Year for the last decade, in fact. But those resolutions had been soon forgotten – 9 January was his record. And what would his friends think when they knew that he had joined the God squad? He imagined the gossip: "Have you heard about John? – he's gone all religious; he's always got a Bible in his hand!" "It's no use," he said. "I could never keep going."

I have spoken to many people like John over the years. Much of my work has been with students from

Oxford University. You might expect that their main difficulties with the Christian faith would be intellectual, but most are satisfied that there is good reason to believe as they have investigated the evidence. The greatest obstacles to these students becoming Christians have been moral. They have recognized that to be a Christian means following Christ as Lord and seeking to go his way through life and many are worried about the changes that will involve. They feel so weak in the face of their own internal desires to do what they know is wrong, and the external peer pressure from their friends. Many say with John, "I could never keep going."

My answer always surprises them: "You are right, you couldn't." On our own we are far too weak to make the changes that are involved in living for Christ. But we are not on our own if we turn to him. The Holy Spirit comes to live in all Christians and it is he who will give us the power to change.

At the time of the great Depression in the 1930s a family of hill-billies was crossing America looking for work. They drove their battered old car through a city in the mid-west. It was the first time they had been to a really big city. Dad was determined to see inside an expensive modern hotel. He stopped the car and went with his son into the foyer of the best hotel in town. Their eyes were agog as they took in the splendour of it all. In the corner was a cubicle. Its doors opened automatically and in walked an old lady with a stick. Somehow the doors closed automatically. Shortly afterwards they opened again and out came a stunningly beautiful young woman with high heels and a tight skirt. Dad's eyes were popping out of his head. He seized his son's arm and, without taking his gaze away from the lift, he said, "Son, go get your ma!"

It is as if God says to us, "Go get your old nature and bring it to the wonder-working God." He has the power to bring transformation and to make something beautiful out of us. Once he comes to live within us he begins to produce his "fruit". Paul wrote that "the fruit of the Spirit is love, joy, peace, patience, kindness, goodness, faithfulness, gentleness and self-control".[22] Those are the qualities that he wants to produce in our lives. He gives us a new desire to live a life that pleases Jesus and the power to put those desires into practice.

That does not mean that we can just sit back and do nothing. As a Christian I am called to make every effort to resist what is wrong and do what is right. But I am not left to do that on my own. It is as I work hard to please Christ that the Spirit gives me the strength I need. An old woodworker from Germany retired and went to live with his son, who had followed in his father's profession. The old man continued to carve bits of wood, but he had lost much of his skill and was upset by his inability to produce the masterpieces for which he had become known. His son did not like seeing his father sad, so every night, after he had gone to bed, he set to work perfecting the carvings. It is a bit like that with the Spirit. He does not do all the work for us. It is as we work that he works. He takes our feeble efforts and adds his own work to them. In that way, bit by bit, we can expect to change and become more like Christ. It does not happen overnight. Christians often fail – our own sinful desires remain very strong. Sometimes we feel as if we are going backwards. But, over time, the change becomes obvious. Many Christians can testify to how God the Spirit has helped them to resist temptation and to begin to be the people that deep down they long to be.

3: He equips God's people to serve him

The prophets had taught that when the Christ came he would introduce the kingdom of God. God's enemies would be punished and his people brought into a perfect relationship with him in a renewed world. It is hardly surprising that expectation was high among the disciples after the resurrection. They knew that Jesus was the promised Messiah, so surely it was just a matter of time before he introduced his kingdom in all its fullness? The book of Acts opens with them in conversation with Jesus. They ask him, "Lord, are you at this time going to restore the kingdom to Israel?"[23] Jesus replies by making it clear that there will be a delay. He will return at an unknown date in the future and it will be then that the kingdom will fully come. Meanwhile, there is work to do: "You will be my witnesses in Jerusalem, and in all Judea and Samaria and to the ends of the earth."[24]

From the beginning God had promised to Abraham that people from all nations would be included in his perfect kingdom. Now is the time for them to be brought in, as the good news about Christ is proclaimed all over the world. That is the reason for the delay in his return – he is giving more people an opportunity to hear about him and put their trust in him that they might be ready when he comes to judge. Peter explained in a letter: "The Lord is not slow in keeping his promise . . . He is patient with you, not wanting anyone to perish, but everyone to come to repentance."[25]

It was a mammoth task for just a few very weak disciples. It can still seem an impossible job today as well. Christians are a small minority in an increasingly indifferent world. It is not easy to stand up and be counted and bear witness to Christ. On our own we never would. But we are not on our own. The command of Christ to his disciples came with a promise: "You will receive power when the Holy Spirit comes on you."[26]

After saying those words, Jesus ascended into heaven and went out of their sight. He will not return until the end of time. The disciples had been told to wait in Jerusalem until the promise was fulfilled and the Spirit was given. That happened at the day of Pentecost. It was no accident that the first thing he did was to enable them to speak about God in other languages. That was a great reminder of why he had been sent – to empower Christians to tell people throughout the world about Christ. They began straight away. On that very day Peter preached and we are told that about 3000 became Christians.[27] The rest of the book of Acts describes the gospel being taken to people all over the Middle East and Europe. That great task continues to this day. Christianity is not a Western religion any more, if it ever was. Hundreds of people are putting their trust in Christ daily in Africa, Asia, Eastern Europe, and indeed in virtually every country in the world. They are receiving the new start that he offers to all who turn to him: life with God that begins here on earth and lasts for ever.

The coming of the Spirit signalled the beginning of what Peter called the "last days" in his speech on the day of Pentecost.[28] This is the age we live in; the time leading up to the second coming in which the gospel is being preached everywhere in the power of the Spirit. The Bible makes it clear that it is a period in which Christians can expect opposition. It will not be easy to live as a Christian and to bear witness to Christ. But God gives us the help we need. Not only does he give us his Spirit, but he also provides the help of other believers. Christians are not meant to be isolated individuals. Christ calls his people to belong to his new community, the church. We need each other. On one occasion Paul calls a church "the body of Christ".[29] Just as the parts of a body are dependent on one another, so individual Christians need the others in a church. We are all given different "gifts" by the Spirit so that we can serve one another and thereby grow to become more mature Christians. We all have a part to play.

The fact that we live in the "last days" means that these are urgent times; Christ could return at any moment. There is an urgency about the need for Christians to take the gospel to all nations. And there is an urgency about the need of those who hear it to respond with faith. Why is that so important? What will happen when Christ comes again? That is the subject of the next chapter.

A History of the World

The story so far:

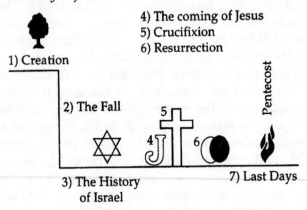

1) Creation

2) The Fall

3) The History of Israel

4) The coming of Jesus
5) Crucifixion
6) Resurrection

7) Last Days

Pentecost

Notes

1. Van Loon, *The Story of Mankind*.
2. Penguin, 1965.
3. Acts 2:3.
4. Acts 2:12.
5. e.g. John 14:17; 16:6.
6. Acts 1:16; 15:28; Ephesians 4:30.
7. John 14:16.
8. John 14:18.
9. Romans 8:9.
10. Ezekiel 36:26–27.
11. Joel 2:28–29.
12. Matthew 27:51; Mark 15:38; Luke 23:45.
13. Acts 2:16–17.
14. 1 Corinthians 6:19.
15. 2 Corinthians 4:4; John 8:34; Ephesians 2:1.
16. John 3:7.
17. John 3:5–6.
18. John 16:8.
19. John 15:26.
20. Matthew 7:7–8.
21. 2 Corinthians 5:17.
22. Galatians 5:22.
23. Acts 1:6.
24. Acts 1:8.
25. 2 Peter 3:9.
26. Acts 1:8.
27. Acts 2:41.
28. Acts 2:17.
29. 1 Corinthians 12.

8

The End and the Beginning

In 1516 Sir Thomas More published a book in which he presented his vision of an idealized England. Throughout history human beings have been dreaming of the perfect world – a world rid of evil, suffering and pain; a world in which all people live together in perfect harmony. More's title has become synonymous with that dream; he called his book *Utopia*.

It was not long ago that many people still believed in it – that "Utopia", "Jerusalem", really could be established on earth, or even be "built here in England's green and pleasant land". The humanists put their trust in the goodness of humanity and in scientific discovery. At the turn of the century there was great hope that all our problems could be solved. But the First World War put a stop to such naïvety and, just in case it still lingered on, the Second World War put the final nail in the coffin. The writer H.G. Wells had been one of the most fervent humanistic optimists. Shortly before he died in 1946 he wrote his final book: *Mind at the End of its Tether*.

The other great utopians of the twentieth century were the Marxists. Here the hope rested on political revolution. If only the workers of the world would unite, a new age of justice, peace and prosperity would be ushered in. Of course, it did not happen. The Marxist dream produced a nightmare, not Utopia.

It is no wonder that ours is a cynical age. More nearly called his book "Nusquam", which is Latin for "Nowhere". In fact the word "Utopia" comes from Greek words meaning either "good place" or "*no* place" – it is just an idle dream. We can long for a perfect world as much as we like, but it will never come. That is the view of most today. We have seen too much in the history of our century to believe such nonsense any more. It is only fairy stories that end with the words, "they lived happily ever after". Utopia is "nowhere", "no place", "never-never land".

The result is a generation that is obsessed with the present because it cannot face the future. "D Ream" might sing that "things can only get better", but no one really believes it. The future is unknown and rather frightening, so we prefer to focus on the here and now. Ours is the age of the instant – instant coffee, instant credit, instant returns. It was summed up in the credit card advert – "Access: Takes the waiting out of wanting". That appeals exactly to our desires. We do not want to have to wait for anything: "I know what I want and I want it now". The only ones who live with their eyes fixed on a vision of the future are fanatics like Jim Jones and David Koresh – cult leaders whose utopian views led their followers to their deaths in Guyana and Waco.

There is the choice that we are left with, as far many are concerned – shut our eyes to the facts and enter the world of make-believe; or face reality head-on and recognize that there is no ultimate hope for the world, no perfect place waiting to be established. But are they the only options? The Bible insists otherwise. It shares much of the pessimism of our generation. It could have shown us the folly of humanism and Marxism long before we learnt that painful lesson through all the evils of the twentieth century. There is no way that we flawed, selfish, sinful human beings will ever establish a perfect world. Even if we could conquer the enemies around us of poverty, disease and decay, we have proved ourselves quite incapable of conquering our greatest enemy – ourselves.

Yes, there is great realism in the Bible, and yet it is combined with tremendous hope. There is a wonderful future to look forward to. Utopia is not just a dream. Heaven will be established. And that is not a foolish hope, because it does not depend on us, but on God. The one who made the universe with a simple word of command has the power to finish it and to establish a new world – a perfect world that will last forever.

Once again, that is not a hope that is blind to reality. The book of "Revelation", which speaks more than any other book in the Bible of the wonder of heaven, was written to Christians who were painfully aware of the wickedness of this world and of human beings in it. They were being severely persecuted for their faith. Christianity is not naïve. It does not refuse to face up to facts of human sin – that was the mistake of humanism and Marxism. No, sin is acknowledged, but it is dealt with. Jesus Christ died to pay the penalty for sin and therein lies our hope. Because of the death and resurrection of Christ we can be sure that God's promise of a perfect world will be fulfilled. It is just a matter of time now until he returns and puts everything right – the end of the world will also be its beginning.

After the American troops were forced to surrender the Philippines to the Japanese in May 1942, General MacArthur vowed to retake the islands. He printed the words "I will return" on thousands of leaflets which were then scattered across the country by aeroplanes. Towards the end of 1944, he kept his promise and the country was liberated soon afterwards. Jesus made his intention to return to earth just as clear. On many occasions he taught that although the date of his coming was a secret, there was no doubt that it would happen: "So you must be ready, because the Son of Man will come at an hour when you least expect him."[1] The second coming of Christ is mentioned over 300 times in the New Testament, an average of once in every thirteen verses.

Jesus taught that when he comes everyone who has ever lived will have to stand before him and be judged. "When the Son of Man comes in his glory, and all the angels with him, he will sit on his throne in heavenly glory. All the nations will be gathered before him, and he will separate the people one from another as a shepherd separates the sheep from the goats".[2] There will be a great division between the wheat and the weeds, the wise and the foolish.[3] Some will go to heaven, others will go to hell.

Hell

There is a little village on the Cayman islands called "Hell". It does very well out of the tourists. Everyone wants to go there so that they can send a postcard from Hell and buy one of the souvenir tee shirts: "I've been to Hell and survived" or "I've been to Hell and my camcorder melted". Hell today is just a joke; few believe that it really exists, except as a village on Grand Cayman. But Jesus took it very seriously. He was the most loving man who ever lived, and yet his teaching is full of references to hell; he spoke about it more than anyone else in the

Bible. But there was no hint that he took any sadistic pleasure in speaking of it. He did so out of love.

A few years ago the sharks had been getting through the barriers and were coming close to the shore off some beaches in Sydney. The authorities put up notices: "Beware of the sharks!" Underneath was a picture of a gruesome shark with vicious teeth. One mother complained that the signs were frightening her children and asked if the shark could be made to look less scary. She had missed the point – those notices were meant to be frightening. Jesus' teaching about hell was designed to have the same effect. He spoke out of a loving concern to warn people about a terrible reality.

1: What is hell?

The Bible uses three main images to describe hell.

Punishment

- Jesus speaks of "eternal punishment" and "eternal fire".[4] Elsewhere he warns: "If your hand causes you to sin, cut it off. It is better to enter life maimed than with two hands to go into hell, where the fire never goes out."[5] It seems that we are not meant to take these images literally; if we do, we find a straight contradiction between fire and darkness, both of which are described as being features of the place and yet which are mutually exclusive. This is picture language, but it portrays a gruesome reality.

Destruction

- Jesus likens some people to branches that are picked up, thrown into the fire and burned. The clear implication is that they are destroyed.[6] The apostle Paul speaks of the punishment of "everlasting destruction".[7] The words "destroy" and "destruction" need not imply that the thing referred to ceases to exist. Elsewhere the disciples use the same word to speak of the "waste" of some ointment that a woman poured on Jesus' head.[8] It still existed, but it had been wasted – it could not be used for anything else. Human beings in hell are destroyed. They are shadows of the glorious beings made in the image of God that they were created to be – shrivelled up, not fully human.

Exclusion

- In the parable of the ten virgins we find that five of them do not go to the wedding feast when the bridegroom, who stands for Jesus, finally comes. He addresses these chilling words to them: "I don't know you", and they are not allowed in.[9] A number of parables describe a similar scene. There will be no gatecrashers in heaven; some will be excluded.

These three images must be held together. The central reality of hell is banishment from God. That is the really terrible thing, not the fire and the darkness, but the absence of God, the source of all that is good in the world. John Donne was not just a great poet but also a fine preacher. In one sermon about hell he said, "When all is done, the hell of hells, the torment of torments, is the everlasting absence of God and the everlasting impossibility of returning into his presence ... To fall out of the hands of the living God is a horror beyond our expression, beyond our imagination."[10] Surely it is that banishment that is so terrible that it can be described in the dreadful imagery of fire and darkness. And it is that same separation from God which leads to destruction as well. Divorced from any relationship with God we cease to be truly human. As C.S. Lewis once put it, "what is cast (or casts itself) into hell is not a man, it is 'remains'".

Perhaps that is as far as we should go. There is inevitably some mystery about the exact nature of hell because, thank God, it is beyond our present experience. We would be wise to be agnostic on some points, but of this we can be clear: it is a terrible reality.

2: How can hell be just?

Why does God not simply forgive us our wrongdoing and have us all in his heaven? We have already considered the answer to a similar question in a previous chapter. Justice demands that wrongdoing is punished. It would be terrible if God just turned his back on the evil in the world and did nothing about it. He would be saying, in effect, that it does not matter; but it does matter. The poet Robert Browning said once, "there may be a heaven, but there must be a hell". He was expressing a widespread sentiment – justice must be seen to be done. The fact of hell proclaims that it will be. And the punishment perfectly fits the crime.

The great crime of humanity is that we choose to live without reference to our maker. The punishment is that God grants us what we wish. C.S. Lewis makes the point in his extended parable, *The Great Divorce*.[11] "There are only two kinds of people in the end; those who say to God, 'Thy will be done', and those to whom God says, in the end, '*Thy* will be done.' All that are in hell choose it." We can hardly complain that it is not fair. God is just confirming for ever the decision that we have made. But is it fair that hell goes on forever? Lewis meets that objection also: "I believe that if a million chances were likely to do any good, they would be given. But a master often knows, when boys and parents do not, that it is really useless to send a boy in for a certain examination again. Finality must come some time, and it does not require a very robust faith to believe that omniscience knows when."[12]

The big question for the Bible is not "Is hell fair?" but "Is forgiveness fair?" How can God forgive people and accept them into his heaven? Does that not involve ignoring what is evil? We saw the answer in chapter 5. On the cross Jesus stood in for others and took their punishment so that all who turn to him can be sure that they are forgiven by God. That is how committed God is to ensuring that we need not face the hell of separation from him which we deserve. It is as if Jesus is saying to us, "You will only go to hell over my dead body." It is because he died that the possibility of heaven is open to us all.

Heaven

The book of Revelation describes a vision that the apostle John was given of the end of time. We read that "He who was seated on the throne said, 'I am making everything new!' "[13] The description of heaven points us to a new creation, new community and new relationship.

1: A new creation

> *Then I saw a new heaven and a new earth, for the first heaven and the first earth had passed away (Revelation 21:1).*

Brian Johnson, the cricket commentator, wrote these words in his autobiography *Someone Who Was* shortly before he died: "I find the after-life an impossible place to imagine or believe in, though I persuade myself that there must be some light at the end of life's dark tunnel. But I do not find it easy to conceive what it might be." He echoes the thoughts of many who like to believe that there is something beyond the grave, but that is all it is – a something. There is no substance to it. It is a world of angels and clouds. If there are any people there, they are disembodied souls floating around in nothingness. The only things with any substance are the harps. It does not exactly sound attractive. Nothing could be further from the Bible's description of heaven. It is not a shadowland. If anything, this present world is the shadowland while heaven is the ultimate reality. It is physical; a real place.

That is hard for us to understand and accept because we are used to such a different view. Often our picture of heaven has more in common with Greek philosophy than the Bible's teaching. For the Greeks, the material world was ultimately bad. In each of us lies a soul, imprisoned within evil matter. Salvation comes when the soul is released and escapes into a non-material world. Similar thinking can be found today in eastern mysticism. But this dislike for the material is not Christian. Matter matters because God made it. He is concerned not just with our souls but with our bodies and the whole material world as well. When we rebelled against God at the Fall it was not just our souls that were affected. There were consequences for our bodies too – disease and death entered the world. And at the same time the whole creation was put out of joint and became "in bondage to decay".[14]

But the great creator's plan of salvation encompasses all that. He has not given up on the world that he has made. He continues to love it and is determined to restore it. The very last chapter of the Bible contains a description of heaven which includes a number of similarities to the Garden of Eden at the very beginning of the Bible. The same key elements are there – a river flowing through and trees next to it. We are meant to spot the significance of that. God has undone the effects of the Fall and restored that perfect garden. Heaven is the perfection of all things, not their end; creation as it was designed to be, before the Fall spoilt it: "a new heaven and a new earth" ("heaven" there refers to the skies). This imperfect creation, the fallen world, will pass away and will be replaced by a perfect new creation which will last for ever. It will be a physical place and those who live there will be physical people. So, if we want to picture heaven we should think of it in terms of the world around us; only, it is better, and more real, not less.

C.S. Lewis puts it brilliantly in the last of his Narnia books. The final chapter is called "Farewell to Shadowlands". Earth is the shadow and heaven is the substance. The children are entering heaven and they are amazed by what they see. It is the same as it had been in Narnia. It is familiar, only better in an indescribable way.

> 'Those hills', said Lucy, 'the nice woody ones and the blue ones behind – aren't they very like the Southern border of Narnia?'
>
> 'Like!' cried Edmund after a moment's silence. 'Why, they're exactly like. Look, there's Mount Pire with his forked head, and there's the pass into Archenland and everything!'
>
> 'And yet they're not like,' said Lucy. 'They're different. They have more colours on them and they look further away than I remembered and they're more. . . . More . . . oh, I don't know . . .'
>
> 'More like the real thing,' said the Lord Digory softly.[15]

2: A new community

> *Then I saw the holy city, the new Jerusalem, coming down out of heaven from God, prepared as a bride beautifully dressed for her husband (Revelation 21:2).*

It is interesting that the picture here is not of people going up to heaven to an ethereal existence. No, heaven is pictured as coming down to earth. It is just as Jesus said it would be: "The meek will inherit the earth."[16] And notice how it is described. It is a city – "the new Jerusalem". There is a surprise. Paradise for many people means escaping the city and finding some beautiful solitary place in the countryside. We want to get away from others. But we need to understand that heaven will be a new community; that is the reality to which the image of the city points.

The Bible challenges the errors both of Eastern mysticism and Western individualism. In heaven I will not be absorbed into the divine and lose my individuality – I will still be a recognizable personality. But I will be an individual in relationship. I cannot expect to pitch my deck chair in a secluded spot, cut off from others. I will live in a community. But it will be a city without all the evils that blight urban life today. There will be no crime, no pollution, no loneliness. It is ironic that the most crowded places on earth, with flats piled on top of each other, are often the loneliest. But in heaven there will be no unwanted isolation. There will be one great happy family, uniting people from "every tribe and language and people and nation".[17]

Jerusalem in the land of Judah, where God lived symbolically in his Temple, was just a shadow of the reality which will be found in heaven. It provides a model which helps us to picture what it will be like, just as, on a larger scale, the whole world is a pale imitation of the renewed creation in heaven.

In the verse quoted at the top of this section John describes the city as "a bride beautifully dressed for her husband". It is a strange mixture of images; we are not used to cities that look like brides. But the description is quite deliberate and underlines the point I have been trying to make. In speaking of heaven as a city, God does not want us to think of tower blocks, shopping centres and roads. He wants us to think of people – a great gathering; a new community which together makes up the bride who will be united in heaven with Jesus Christ, the great bridegroom. Once again we see that God is not simply calling a collection of individuals to himself. He calls a people who belong together and to him.

3: A new relationship

> *And I heard a loud voice from the throne saying, 'Now the dwelling of God is with men, and he will live with them. They will be his people, and God himself will be with them and be their God (Revelation 21:3).*

A few years ago a charity asked celebrities to describe their idea of heaven for a book. Princess Anne said that, for her, it was sailing with friends on a summer's day. Jeffrey Archer spoke of an eternal game of cricket. For some that sounds like hell, but I can begin to identify with it. If you had been asked to contribute, what would you have said? Perhaps you would have mentioned a favourite place, or pastime, or person. Those things may or may not be in heaven, but they are not what dominates the Bible's vision. The fundamental reality of heaven is that it is where God is. That is what should excite the Christian about going there. At the moment "we live by faith, not by sight."[18] But then we will see him and enjoy a perfect relationship with him.

That was the mark of the Garden of Eden. Adam and Eve lived there in fellowship with their creator. But those days are gone; the Fall put a stop to all that. And, ever since, there has been a separation between God and humanity. God does not live here on earth. That is why things are not as they should be. Ours is a world that is under the judgement of God because of our rebellion against him. We have turned away from him and, as a result, he has turned away from us.

That is where God could have left us – cut off from him. But in his great love he longs for relationship with us. He appeared to Abraham and promised to bless his descendants, the people of Israel and, through them, all the nations of the world. He said that he would be their God and they would be his people.

That promise was partially fulfilled in the history of Israel in the Old Testament. God called them to himself and drew close to them, living in the Temple in their midst. But, as we have seen, it was still a fairly distant relationship. The problem was the sin of the people. It was only once that barrier had been removed by the death of Jesus on the cross that it was possible for the promise to Abraham to be completely fulfilled. All those who trust in Christ can now know God by his Spirit who comes to live within them. But still it is an incomplete relationship. By the Spirit we have, in this fallen world, just a taste of what it is to know God and be known by him, but there is so much more to be enjoyed. Paul said, "Now we see but a poor reflection as in a mirror; then we shall see face to face. Now I know in part; then I shall know fully, even as I am fully known."[19]

John writes in the book of Revelation:

> No longer will there be any curse. The throne of God and of the lamb will be in the city, and his servants will serve him. They will see his face, and his name will be on their foreheads. There will be no more night. They will not need the light of a lamp or the light of the sun, for the Lord God will give them light and they will reign for ever and ever.[20]

The "curse" refers to the judgement of God on human sin. It has no place in heaven because Jesus has already faced it in the place of all who are there. As a result, they can stand before God. At the centre of heaven is God's throne, a reminder of his presence and reign. It is very striking that the "lamb" sits on it. That is a reference to Jesus, who died as a sacrificial lamb. It was by his death that he achieved the great victory that made the new creation possible. Around the throne stand God's people, enjoying the perfect light of his radiance. John tells us that there is no temple in heaven. There is no need for one – the whole place is filled with the presence of God.

Do you remember the question with which this book began: "Is history ordered or random?" That is not just a matter for academics to discuss; it has great relevance for each one of us. If human history is a random process, going nowhere, then life has no meaning; and we can have little hope as we enter a new millennium. The last thousand years have seen great progress in many fields, but the human heart has remained unchanged – still capable of terrible evil. But history is not random; it is governed by a sovereign God. He has already acted to work out his loving purposes, and one day he will bring them to their ultimate fulfilment.

Then, at last, the effects of the Fall will have been undone. With God restored to the centre of his creation, everything can be put right. "He will wipe every tear from their eyes. There will be no more death or mourning or crying or pain, for the old order of things has passed away."[21] What a wonderful thought that is!

I am writing on the day when 16 of the 28 victims of the terrible bomb at Omagh in Northern Ireland are being buried. Once more we see the anguish of the bereaved, tears streaming down their faces; the confusion of little children, left without mother, uncle, brother, friend; the despair of the people. But such things will not go on forever. God is faithful; he always does what he says he will do. He will appear to fulfil his promises and introduce his kingdom in all its fullness, which was made possible by the death and resurrection of Christ. Utopia is no idle dream; it is reality, because it depends not on human effort but on God. The Bible closes with a reassurance: "Yes, I am coming soon." And God's people respond: "Amen. Come, Lord Jesus."[22]

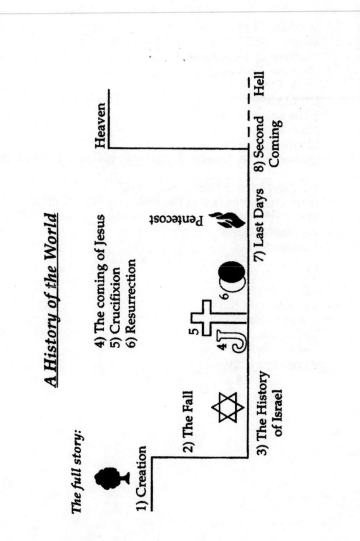

A History of the World

The full story:

1) Creation

2) The Fall

3) The History of Israel

4) The coming of Jesus
5) Crucifixion
6) Resurrection

Pentecost

7) Last Days

8) Second Coming

Heaven

Hell

Notes

1. Matthew 24:44.
2. Matthew 25:31–32.
3. Matthew 25:1–13; 13:24–30.
4. Matthew 25:41, 46.
5. Mark 9:43.
6. John 15:6.
7. 2 Thessalonians 1:9.
8. Mark 14:4.
9. Matthew 25:1–13.
10. Quoted in D.A. Carson, *The Gagging of God*, (Apollos, 1996), 53.
11. *The Great Divorce* (Bles, 1946), 66–67.
12. In the chapter on hell in *The Problem of Pain* (Fontana, 1957), 112.
13. Revelation 21:5.
14. Romans 8:21.
15. C.S. Lewis, *The Last Battle* (Puffin, 1964), 152–3.
16. Matthew 5:5.
17. Revelation 5:9.
18. 2 Corinthians 5:7.
19. 1 Corinthians 13:12.
20. Revelation 22:3–5.
21. Revelation 21:4.
22. Revelation 22:20.

9

Turning Point

A boy in his later teens knelt at his bedside one Sunday night . . . In a simple matter-of-fact but definite way he told Christ that he had made rather a mess of life so far; he confessed his sins; he thanked Christ for dying for him; and he asked him to come into his life. The following day he wrote in his diary: 'Yesterday really was an eventful day! . . . Up till now Christ has been on the circumference and I have asked him to guide me instead of giving him complete control. Behold he stands at the door and knocks. I have heard him and now he has come into my house. He has cleansed it and now rules in it.'

And the day after:

'I really have felt an immense and new joy throughout today. It is the joy of being at peace with the world and of being in touch with God. How well do I know now that he rules me and that I never really knew him before.'[1]

A young woman found herself on a weekend with a group of Christians. She had been reading the Bible and thinking about the Christian faith for a while. She later described what happened next:

> My mind went back . . . through the past term and the multitude of new influences and new friendships, back to my home and family and childhood. Suddenly, I flung myself on my bed in a flood of tears and loneliness. With an overwhelming sense of failure and helplessness I cried out to God (if there was a God) to meet with me and make utterly real and vital to me *Himself*. I raised my eyes, and through my tears I read a text on the wall: 'Be still and know that I am God' (Psalm 46:10). That was all. Immediately the whole burden fell away in a moment. Be still and know God, whose name is 'I am'. Be still and know Him. Stop going to this one and that; stop striving to understand with the intellect. Just be still, and *know Him*. In that moment, a great flood of peace and joy and unutterable happiness flooded in, and I knew that He and I had entered into a relationship. I knew God, and I *knew* in that moment that all the theories were true, and somehow He would work them out for me . . . For years the Holy Spirit had been opening my eyes to a sense of sin, convicting me of my unworthiness before a Holy God. But now came the wonderful gift of repentance. God poured out His grace in forgiveness, in cleansing from all the uncleanness of sin, and in revealing, at this time, the amazing wonder of the friendship of Christ.[2]

A young atheist could only remember one prayer that he prayed during his time in the army: "After an especially wild party and while lying on my bed still dressed in my dinner jacket, and with a powerful hangover, I said aloud, 'O God, there must be a better life somewhere!' " He never imagined that that drunken heart-cry would be answered through a meeting that some Christian friends invited him to attend. The talk got him thinking so when the speaker suggested that they meet for breakfast the next day, he agreed. Their conversation was to revolutionize his life. "Off I went with my mind racing. I had gone to breakfast as a humanist, and now, just an hour or so later, I had the trembling excitement that I could be on the verge of a totally unexpected discovery. Or again, it could be yet another disillusionment which would only deepen my conviction as an atheist." He read a booklet he had been given which outlined how he could make a start in the Christian life:

> Steadily I realised that, if these things were true, I wanted them to become real in my own life. Awkwardly I slipped onto my knees beside my bed and prayed the prayer at the end of the booklet . . . Absolutely nothing happened. No visions, no feelings, no experiences, nothing. Everything seemed just the same as before. I felt let down; and yet as I climbed into bed I had a quiet sense of peace that I had done the right thing.[3]

These are three individuals describing the turning point of their lives as they accepted Christ for themselves. The time has come to think about where we fit into the history of the world as it is presented in the Bible. We have seen that it is not a random process, heading nowhere. This world had a definite beginning and will have a definite end. God made everything and one day, when Christ returns, he will bring it to a close. But that will not be the end of history. It will mark the beginning of a new creation, unspoilt and everlasting. We have a chance to be part of that perfect world and not face the judgement that we deserve.

In some words recorded in the Gospels, Christ speaks to us and invites us to follow him, so that in these "last days" we might be ready for his return:

> Then he called the crowd to him along with his disciples and said: 'If anyone would come after me, he must deny himself and take up his cross and follow me. For whoever wants to save his life will lose it, but whoever loses his life for me and for the gospel will save it. What good is it for a man to gain the whole world, yet forfeit his soul? Or what can a man give in exchange for his soul? If anyone is ashamed of me and my words in this adulterous and sinful generation, the Son of Man will be ashamed of him when he comes in his Father's glory with the holy angels (Mark 8:34–37).

An invitation

We find in these words two invitations:

1: An invitation to die

Dietrich Bonhoeffer was a German Christian leader, hanged by the Nazis during the war. He said once: "When Christ calls a man, he bids him come and die." That is what we see in Jesus' words: "If anyone would come after me, he must deny himself and take up his cross and follow me." The Polar explorer Ernest Shackleton placed an advert in the London papers at the turn of the century inviting people to join him on one of his expeditions. It said: "Men wanted for hazardous journey. Small wages; bitter cold; long months in complete darkness; constant danger; safe return doubtful." He did not get many applicants! One wonders how much emptier churches would be if we advertised for Christian converts in similar terms. But Jesus did! He invited people to join him on a hazardous adventure. We do not hear much of that today. We have managed to do something that the early Christians would not have thought possible. We have made Christianity safe, middle-class, comfortable. Even when we acknowledge these words of Jesus, we tame them. So, self-denial becomes giving up sugar in Lent and taking up our cross means enduring back pain or having Aunt Agatha to stay at Christmas. But the words of Jesus go far deeper than that. The only ones in Palestine who were seen carrying crosses were those on their way to be executed. Jesus is saying "You must be willing to die for me. You too must be willing to go the way of the cross."

That is a long way from the popular conception of the Christian life; this is not for wimps. For a long time I thought that Christianity was all about being religious – becoming a choir boy and going to one church service after another. It did not appeal then and, to be honest, it does not appeal now. But there is none of that in Jesus' teaching. To be a Christian is not to become religious; it is to die for Christ.

What does that mean in practice? Put very simply, it means putting him above ourselves. We all have an instinct for self-preservation and self-promotion. We will do almost anything to protect ourselves from harm and to promote our happiness, image and reputation. In the language of Jesus, it is the desire to "save our lives". And he calls on us to place that instinct for self-preservation and self-promotion beneath a higher loyalty – a desire to follow him. We are to be willing to lose our lives for him; to do things for him which may not be in the interests of our health, immediate happiness or reputation. Sometimes that does mean literal death. There have been more martyrs this century than in all the other centuries of Christian history put together. But it is very unlikely that we will have to face that. And yet, in less dramatic ways Christ invites us all to deny ourselves and take up our crosses; to say 'yes' to him and 'no' to ourselves when there is a clash between the two.

Let us suppose that you have just made a start as a Christian. You are with a group of friends when one of them starts dismissing Christianity: "No one in their right minds believes that nonsense any more!" Do you stay silent, not wanting to risk your reputation with your friends, or do you admit that you believe it? In the language of Christ, do you "save your life" or do you "lose it"? Or you are at a party. Everyone is getting drunk and pairing off. Which comes first: Christ or your own desires? Or perhaps you are in the canteen at lunch time. Everyone is enjoying a character assassination of someone who is not there. Do you add your own verbal dagger or, for the sake of Christ who calls his disciples to follow his example of love, do you keep silent, or even say something positive?

I could go on and on. In every area of our lives there are conflicts between what we want and how Christ would have us live. Often we know that his way is best, but will we follow it? If we do, he wants us to be in no doubt that that will be hard. It may well be that some will laugh at us. There will certainly be things in our lives that are wrong, which we will have to stop; and other things that we will have to start doing. It will not be easy being a Christian; it involves going the way of self-denial, the way of the cross. Jesus offers an invitation to die: "If anyone would come after me, he must deny himself and take up his cross and follow me."

It all sounds a bit gloomy so far. How could it ever be worthwhile following Christ? We need to consider the other side to the invitation.

2: An invitation to live

The stakes are high according to Jesus. If we choose to "save our lives" and put ourselves first, not him, we will end up losing them. We will miss out on life in relationship with God here on earth and for eternity. Many feel that it is much wiser not to be a Christian – surely we will have much more fun that way? After all, we have got to look after number one haven't we? But Jesus says, "What good is it for a man to gain the whole world, yet forfeit his soul?" Those who reject Christ because they want to cling on to their popularity, or some cherished sin, or their independence, end up losing everything. This world is not all there is. Jesus is coming again and we will all have to stand before him as our judge. He says some solemn words: "If anyone is ashamed of me and my words in this adulterous and sinful generation, the Son of Man will be ashamed of him when he comes in his Father's glory with the holy angels." If we choose to save our lives and refuse to hand them over to Jesus, we will lose them. "But," says Jesus, "whoever loses his life for me and for the gospel will save it." Just as he went from the cross to the resurrection, so he invites us to travel via death to life. The paradox is that it is only as we are willing to "die", or hand over our lives to Christ, that we experience life.

That, ultimately, is what Jesus offers us: life; "eternal life", as the Bible calls it. That refers not so much to quantity of life (life that goes on and on forever) as to quality of life – life as it was designed to be lived, in relationship with God, which happens to go on forever. I will consider in more detail in the epilogue just what that involves. Jesus called it "fullness of life".[4] In brief, it means that we can live now in the knowledge that we are loved by God, have been forgiven by him and accepted into his family. We can experience the great privilege of God the Holy Spirit at work in our lives assuring us of our new status and giving us hope for the future. And one day we can be sure of life with God in the perfect world that he will make. I have been a Christian for fifteen years now. It has not always been easy, but I have never regretted the decision I made to follow Christ, not once. I have not lost my individuality; in fact Christ has set me free to begin to be the person that I long to be. Even in this fallen world I have been given a joy and peace that surpass anything I had before, and that is as nothing to the life I will one day enjoy forever. So, the Christian is actually very wise. A young man, who was killed for his faith in his early twenties, put it well: "He is no fool who gives what he cannot keep, to gain what he cannot lose."

What should I do?

It is decision time. We have been considering a message that claims to make sense of the whole of human history. If true, its implications for each of us are enormous. You are likely to make a number of important decisions in your life, such as who you will marry and what job you will do, but you will never make a more important decision than this. The Bible's claim is that your eternal destiny depends on how you respond to Jesus Christ – this is a matter of life and death.

There are a number of different responses that you can make. Perhaps you are still not convinced. You may feel that there is more to Christianity than you had previously thought, but all sorts of questions remain in your mind. If so, ask them. It will do your Christian friends a lot of good to be put on the spot. But be honest with yourself. Are your questions real obstacles to faith or are they just an excuse to delay?

The story is told of three junior devils who were set one question in their finals exam: "What would you do to persuade someone who has been thinking about Jesus not to become a Christian?" The first devil thought for a while and then he wrote, "I would tell him that there is no God." The senior devil gave him 20 per cent – FAIL – and wrote at the bottom of the paper, "That might persuade a few people here and there, but deep down everyone knows that there is a God." The next devil wrote, "I would tell him that there is no judgement." He got 30 per cent – FAIL – "There are some hardened consciences out there, but almost everyone is aware that they are accountable." The final devil simply wrote, "I would tell him that there is no hurry." He got the top first.

Many people begin to think about the Christian faith and are even strongly challenged by it, but then they get busy and push it to the back of their minds. They may say to themselves, "I'll think about it again when finals are out of the way, or once it's less busy at work," but the reality is that they never get round to it. That is a big mistake. These things are too important to push into the background. Wherever you stand after reading this book, make sure that you go on to the next step, whatever that might be.

It may be that you are convinced that what we have been considering is true. You agree that Jesus was the one promised in the Old Testament Scriptures who by his death and resurrection changed the course of eternal history. But now you are asking, "What should I do?" "How can I become a Christian myself?" Once again we will look to some words of Jesus for the answer. As he began his public ministry he declared: "The time has come. The kingdom of God is near. Repent and believe the good news!"[5]

We have seen that Jesus came to earth to establish the kingdom of God. His death made it possible for us to be reconciled to God on earth and to have a certain hope of being part of his kingdom when it is established at the end of time. But we do not enter that kingdom automatically. Jesus tells us what we need to do – we must repent and believe.

1: Repent

To repent means more than shedding crocodile tears of remorse. It literally means to "turn around"; it involves changing direction. By nature we all live as if we are in control. We are the bosses of our lives; we do what we want. But we have seen that in fact Jesus is the king of the universe; he is the great God who should come first in our lives. We are guilty of a dreadful crime in rejecting him and we need to repent.

A few months ago I set out in my car to go to London. It had been a busy week and I slipped into autopilot mode and drove the familiar route without really thinking about it. It was only when I passed a sign marked "Banbury" that I realized that I was heading towards Birmingham in completely the wrong direction. I suppose I could have carried on and saved myself the embarrassment of admitting to myself that I had made a mistake, but it would not have changed the fact that I was going the wrong way. In the end I did the only sensible thing – I got off the motorway at the next exit and turned round.

In the same way, we need to recognize that we have made a mistake and change the direction of our lives. Christ calls on us to stop going our own way through they would like to believe, but they are just not that type – they were not born like that. But faith is not just the preserve of a few – all of us exercise faith every day of our lives. In essence, to believe means to "trust". Whenever someone makes a claim, we have to choose whether or not we will trust their word. Suppose I say to you, "I will give you £5000 if you come to my house at six o'clock this evening." You may think that I am just having you on, in which case you will ignore what I have said and stay at home. On the other hand, you may trust what I say; in which case you will be knocking on my door as soon as it is six o'clock. That is faith.

We have a similar choice to make about the gospel of Christ. He says to us that as God's Son he is able to forgive us if we trust in him. We can reject that claim or we can believe it. And if we believe it, we are bound to do something about it. It would be very strange if you told me that you really believed that I would give you £5000 if you came to my house, while making no effort to come. Faith must involve action. In a similar way, if you believe that Jesus can forgive you and put you right with God his Father, you are bound to come to him and ask him for that forgiveness.

Are you ready to take that step? Perhaps you are not sure whether you have put your trust in Christ before or not. In which case, can I encourage you to make sure; as it were, to go over in ink what you may already have written in pencil. Or it may be that you know that you have never come to Christ, but you have been conscious as you have been reading this book that God is calling you. If so, do not delay; God's time is always today. The Bible often stresses that point: "Seek the Lord while he may be found; call on him while he is near"; "Today, if you hear his voice, do not harden your hearts"; "Now is the time of God's favour, now is the day of salvation."[6]

I suggest that you take a moment on your own to pray. It might seem strange at first, but remember that God is with you and hears everything you say to him. Say sorry for the way in which you have disobeyed him and tell him that you want to repent – to turn around and put him first in your life from now on. Then thank him for sending Jesus to die that you might be forgiven. Tell him that you believe that his death was for you and that you trust in him.

You might find it helpful to use this prayer and to make it your own:

> *Lord God, my creator, I confess that I have not put you first in my life. I do not deserve anything from you except your anger. But now I repent. I do not want to live for myself any more; I want to serve Jesus as my Lord. I thank you for sending him to die on the cross. I believe and trust that he died for me. Please come into my life now by your Holy Spirit and enable me to live for Jesus for the rest of my life and then to be with him for ever in heaven. Amen.*

If you have prayed that prayer and meant it, you can be sure that God has heard and answered. The Bible says, "To all who received him, to those who believed in his name, he gave the right to become children of God."[7] Jesus himself said, "Whoever comes to me I will never drive away."[8] Do not put your trust in your feelings – they will go up and down. Trust rather in God's promise. Throughout this book we have seen how God keeps his promises. He could have turned his back on humanity after the Fall, but he loves us too much for that. He promised to Abraham that he would act to restore a people to himself; and he did. He promised through the prophets that he would send his Messiah; and he did. He promised that he would raise Jesus from the dead;

Notes

1. John Stott, *Basic Christianity* (IVP, 1958), 128.
2. Helen Roseveare, *Give Me This Mountain* (IVP, 1966), 33–34.
3. David Watson, *You are My God* (Hodder, 1983), 21–22.
4. John 10:10.
5. Mark 1:15.
6. Isaiah 55:6; Psalm 95:7; 2 Corinthians 6:2.
7. John 1:12.
8. John 6:37.
9. Revelation 22:20.

Epilogue

What now?

These last few pages are written for anyone who prayed
the prayer in the previous chapter and has just begun
the Christian life. No doubt you are asking the question,
"What happens next?" You have begun a whole new life
and you will need help. Perhaps the best thing you can
do to start with is tell someone – a Christian friend who
is a bit further down the road and can assist you along
the way. There will be many changes. Here are a few of
them:

A new Father

> *How great is the love the Father has lavished on us, that we*
> *should be called children of God! (1 John 3:1).*

At the funeral of Sir Matt Busby, a former manager of
Manchester United, Busby's son turned to George Best,
the footballer, and said, "You know, he always thought
of you as a son." Best replied, "I am not worthy to be the

son of such a great man." How much more is that true of us with God! And yet, if we have trusted in Christ, we can be sure that God is indeed our Father. Unlike some human fathers, he loves us and is totally committed to us.

All relationships depend on communication, and that is also true of our relationship with our heavenly Father. If we are to grow in our knowledge and love of him it is important that we keep in contact with him. He speaks to us as we read his word, the Bible, and we can speak to him through prayer. Get hold of a modern translation of the Bible if you have not got one. Try to put aside a few minutes every day to read a short passage. You could start with one of the Gospels. Many Christians follow Bible reading notes which suggest a section to read and give some comments about it.[1] Start by praying that God would help you understand what he is saying. Then close by praying again, asking for help to put into practice what you have learnt. You could also pray for one or two friends and for your own personal needs. Remember that God is your Father. He is concerned about every detail of your life. You can speak to him wherever you are and at any time, thanking him, praising him, saying sorry and asking for things.

A new lifestyle

> *I urge you, brothers, in view of God's mercy, to offer your bodies as living sacrifices . . . Do not conform any more to the pattern of this world, but be transformed by the renewing of your mind (Romans 12:1–2).*

No one will ever be made right with God by being a good person – we are not good compared to God's perfection. Our only hope is in the mercy of God. We depend not on what we do but on what Christ has done for us on the cross. But that does not mean that we are free to do whatever we want. We are called to follow the way of Christ, which will mean living a very different way to those around us. We are not to copy "the pattern of this world". As Christians we belong to the world to come. Our values are those of heaven, not of this fallen world. We need to read the Bible to see how God wants us to live. In that way our minds will be "renewed" and we will increasingly see how we should behave. There will be implications for every area of life: how we behave at home, in the office or lecture theatre, at the party or on the sports field; how we treat our superiors, the opposite sex, the unpopular and the homeless.

It will not be easy. It has been said that even a dead dog can swim with the tide. It is much harder to go against it. That is what we are called to do. Paul adds to the appeal by reminding us of what Christ has done for us. It is "in view of God's mercy" that we are to offer ourselves to his service. Gratitude is the prime motivation for Christian obedience.

There will be so many areas of our lives that will need to change that it is very hard to know where to start. Many have found that it helps to concentrate on one thing at a time, asking for God's help to go his way. However hard we try, it is inevitable that we will fail at times. The old sinful desires remain very strong and will be with us throughout our lives on earth. Do not let your failures blow you off course. Remember that your relationship with God does not depend on you being a good person but rather on the death of Christ. He died for all your sins – past, present and future. When you do something wrong, say sorry and thank God again for the cross which ensures that you have been forgiven by

God. Then pick yourself up and try once more to live a
life that pleases him.

A new enemy

> *Your enemy the devil prowls around like a roaring lion looking
> for someone to devour (1 Peter 5:8).*

The moment we start to follow Christ we have a new
enemy. The devil has been defeated by Christ on the
cross. The result of the spiritual battle is not in doubt,
but he has not laid down his arms. It will only be when
Christ returns that he will be destroyed forever.
Meanwhile he continues to fight against God and his
people. We should not be surprised that the Christian
life feels like a battle sometimes. The devil will do all he
can to persuade us to disobey Christ. But we need not
fear. On our own we could never resist the devil's
power, but we are not on our own; we have a new com-
panion.

A new companion

> *He who is in you is stronger than he who is in the world (1
> John 4:4).*

The Holy Spirit enters the lives of all who turn to Christ.
We do not see him, but that does not mean that we cannot believe that he is there. When I was a student I never
saw the postman – I got up long after he had come. But
I still believed that he existed because I saw the evidence
– the letters appeared every morning. We can believe
that the Spirit is in our lives because we see the evidence

of his presence. Have we recognized our need of Christ and turned to him? We could never have come to believe in Christ if the Spirit had not enabled us to. And do we long to live Christ's way? That has also been given to us by the Spirit. He gives us both new desires and the power to carry them out, despite the devil's attempts to stop us. So, when we feel tempted, we should pray to God and ask him to help us by his Holy Spirit. It does not matter where we are – on the sports field, in the bar, at the office, he is there with us and can give us the power we need.

A new family

> Let us consider how we may spur one another on towards love and good deeds. Let us not give up meeting together, as some are in the habit of doing, but let us encourage one another – and all the more as you see the day approaching (Hebrews 10:24–25).

Someone once said to me, "I don't need to go to church to be a Christian." He was right, of course. Being a Christian is not ultimately about going to church services on a Sunday; it is knowing Jesus Christ and trying to live for him seven days a week. But it would be very strange for one who was trying to do that not to want to meet with others with the same goal in life. In fact it would be to disobey God, who tells us that we should meet together. The Bible knows nothing of solitary Christianity. When God calls us to be his children we become, at the same time, brothers and sisters of all his other children; we belong to a new family. As those who belong to heaven, we find that we are strangers and foreigners in this world. We are in a minority and need all the help we can get from others like us. Therefore get involved with a local church. Look for one where the Bible is taught and the good news about Jesus is preached. You will find that they are a strange collection of people and it may take a while to feel that you belong, but what unites you as Christians is far more important than any superficial differences there may be. You will find that the support of other Christians is invaluable to you as you make a start in the Christian life. But the relationships should not be one-way. Before long you will need to be thinking about what you could do for them.

The Bible teaches that all those who belong to Christ should be baptized. Baptism is the symbol that marks someone out as a follower of Christ. It will remind you of the new life and forgiveness that God has given you, and provide an opportunity for you to "go public" as a Christian. All churches encourage new Christians to be baptized. Practice differs for those who have already been baptized, perhaps as an infant.

A new hope

> *Praise be to the God and Father of our Lord Jesus Christ! In his great mercy he has given us new birth into a living hope through the resurrection of Jesus Christ from the dead, and into an inheritance that can never perish, spoil or fade – kept in heaven for you (1 Peter 1:3–4).*

As Christians we are waiting people who have not yet received all that has been promised. We still live in this fallen world and can expect to experience our share of its suffering. We will get sick, fail exams, lose our jobs and face bereavement along with everyone else. What we have already received from Christ is marvellous – the forgiveness of sins, friendship with God by the Holy Spirit and the fellowship of other believers; but all that is as nothing compared to what we will receive in heaven. Then at last we will be able to enjoy life as it is meant to be lived, without everything that spoils this present world. There will be none of the awful "S's": no sin; no Satan; no sadness; no sickness; no separation; no suffering. When hard times come we should set our sights on the glorious future that God has promised us.

A new job

> *Go and make disciples of all nations, baptising them in the name of the Father and of the Son and of the Holy Spirit, and teaching them to obey everything I have commanded you. And surely I will be with you to the very end of the age (Matthew 28:19–20).*

Just before he ascended into heaven, Christ gave his final instructions to his followers. That command is sometimes referred to as "the great commission". It makes it very clear what our job should be in these "last days" leading up to the second coming of Christ. The reason he has delayed his return is to make it possible for more people to be ready for him and to be with him for ever in heaven. It is the gospel that will make them ready, as they hear the good news about Jesus and put their trust in him. And we have been entrusted with the privilege of spreading that message to "all nations".

What part does God want you to play in that great task? It may be that in years to come you should be doing some kind of paid Christian work. We will not all be preaching to crowds or missionaries overseas, but we all have a part to play. You are to be a witness to Jesus amongst your family, friends and colleagues. At first it is your life that will count the most. Many Christians would say that it was the Christ-like life of a friend that first prompted them to think about the Christian message. Then look for opportunities to speak about Christ or to invite your friends to hear a talk at church. Be very careful at home – unwise words too quickly said can alienate close family members more than they attract them. And, all the time, pray. Are there two or three friends close to you for whom you could pray regularly? Remember, in the end it will be God who will draw them to Christ and not your fine arguments.

We have come a long way from the creation in chapter 1. The Fall spoilt everything, but the loving God did not leave us there. He promised to put all things right again, and to call a people to himself who would enjoy life for ever in his restored world, heaven. The fulfilment of that great promise has been made possible by the death and resurrection of Christ. If we belong to him we can be sure that we will enjoy that wonderful future. Meanwhile, as we wait for his return, it is our privilege to bear witness to him by the way we live and by what we say.

If all that sounds a bit frightening, take to heart the encouraging words with which Jesus ended his command: "Surely I am with you always, to the very end of the age." "The end of the age" refers to his return, when he will bring this present world to an end and introduce a new heaven and a new earth. We do not know when that will be, and we have been warned that there will be hard times before it happens. But through them all, we can be sure of the presence of Christ by his Holy Spirit strengthening us and spurring us on.